The Aga Khan Award for Architecture

The Aga Khan Award for Architecture

MODERNITY AND COMMUNITY: ARCHITECTURE IN THE ISLAMIC WORLD

–

–

–

WITH 296 ILLUSTRATIONS, 82 IN COLOR

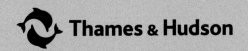 Thames & Hudson

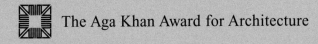 The Aga Khan Award for Architecture

Acknowledgments

This monograph was conceived and directed under the guidance of the members of the 2001 Award Steering Committee. Descriptions of the winning projects are based on the written reports of the technical reviewers who visited each project on site. Design and layout of the book were undertaken by Armand Mevis and Linda van Deursen (Mevis en van Deursen, Amsterdam), Lucas Dietrich coordinated the publication at Thames & Hudson, and Philippa Baker edited the texts. Special thanks to H. Peter Dusk.

First published in paperback in the United States of America in 2002 by Thames & Hudson Inc., 500 Fifth Avenue, New York, New York 10110

Library of Congress Catalog Number 2001094764
ISBN 0-500-28330-3

Designed by Mevis en van Deursen, Amsterdam
Printed and bound in the United Kingdom by Butler and Tanner

Photo Credits

(L: left, R: right, B: bottom, TR: top right, TL: top left, BR: bottom right, BL: bottom left, M: middle)

Kamran Adle: 140 L; Geoffrey Bawa: 18, 19, 20; Jacques Bétant: 172; Hélène Binet: 16, 21, 22–23, 24–25, 26, 41, 42–43, 44, 45, 46, 47; Christoph Bon: 27 TR, 27 B; Courtesy of Geoffrey Bawa: 28 TL, 29, 32 L, 48; Courtesy of the Barefoot College: 79, 81, 82 T, 85B; Chana Daswatte: 36 TL; Cemal Emden:14 M, 126–36; Seiichi Furuya: 117–24; Barry Iverson: 102, 104; Kamran Jebreili: 138; Sian Kennedy: 13 R, 90, 92; Aglaia Konrad: 15, 105–12; Albert Lim K S: 14 T, 150, 151, 152 BL, 153, 154, 156–60; Rahul Mehrotra: 152 T, 155 BR; Samir Natour: 114; Gholamreza Pasban Hazrat: 140 R; Urik Plesner: 27 TL; Christian Richters: 30, 31, 32 R, 33, 34, 35, 37 TR, 38, 39; David Robson: 28 R, 28B, 36 TL, 36B, 37 TL; Samir Saddi: 13 L, 115; Hans Scholten: 11, 66–76; Johannes Schwartz: 11 T, 54–64; Nigel Shafran: 14 B, 139, 141-148; Onerva Utriainen: 91, 93–100; Rajesh Vora: 78, 80, 82 BL, 83, 84, 85 T, 86–88

Pages 163-170
Kamran Adle, Mohammad Akram, Hana Alamuddin, Mokhless Al-Hariri, Gregorius Antar, Chant Avedissian, Jacques Bétant, Timothy Bradley, Steven Cohn, Courtesy of A. Abdelhalim, Courtesy of Abdel Wahid El-Wakil, Courtesy of Arriyadh Development Authority, Courtesy of Saleh Lamei-Mostafa, Courtesy of Skidmore Owings & Merrill, Argun Dundar, Abdel Wahed El-Wakil, Cemal Emden, Monica Fritz, Reha Günay, Güven Incirlioglu, Barry Iverson, Jan Olav Jensen, Christian Lignon, Christopher Little, Pascal Maréchaux, Khedija M'Hadhebi, Kamel Nefzi, K L Ng, Suha Özkan, John Paniker, Jacques Perez, Ram Rahman, Samir Saddi

Drawings
Provided by the architects and redrawn by Darab Diba with Houshang Amir Ardalan

The Aga Khan Award for Architecture

CONTENTS

The objective of the Aga Khan Award for Architecture is to enhance the practice and understanding of architecture in Islamic societies. Since it was founded, the Award has brought to architects and clients a heightened awareness of architectural history and cultural specificity, of place and climate, and of building materials and construction techniques. Through the example of distinguished completed projects, the Award promotes the creation and maintenance of built environments that assure social, cultural and environmental well-being.

The Award is organized on the basis of a three-year cycle, and is governed by a Steering Committee, chaired by His Highness the Aga Khan. Prizes totalling up to US$ 500,000 – the largest architectural award in the world – are shared among projects selected by an independent, multidisciplinary Master Jury. The Award has completed seven cycles of activity since 1977. The current, eighth, cycle covers the period from 1999 to 2001.

The procedures of the Award seek to identify qualities of design excellence, cultural awareness and social and economic responsiveness. There are no overriding or absolute standards against which the winning projects can be measured, but the understanding that architecture has a social contract has been at the heart of the Award's mission. The projects must, however, meet several fixed criteria. For example, all projects must have been completed and in use for a minimum period of one year and a maximum period of twelve years. The focus of the Award is on Islamic societies, and the winning projects must be intended to serve a significant percentage of Muslims. Projects identified to receive Awards are expected to demonstrate a high standard of excellence.

The Award is unique in its procedures because projects shortlisted by each Master Jury are examined on site by Technical Reviewers, according to the Jury's brief for further information and for a critical assessment of use and the project's fulfilment – or failure to fulfil – its programme. These procedures ensure that the Jury can make informed decisions, rather than relying upon limited visual presentations alone. The Master Jury's rigour of selection and independence of choice are thus safeguarded and ensured. In the review of projects, and in the final selection of Award recipients, the Master Jury is fully autonomous and independent, and its decisions are final.

The special Chairman's Award was established to honour achievements that fall outside the scope of the Master Jury's mandate, and is made by the Aga Khan on the recommendation of the Steering Committee, in recognition of the lifetime achievements of distinguished architects.

The Aga Khan Award for Architecture was established in 1977 by His Highness the Aga Khan, the forty-ninth hereditary *Imam* of the Shia Ismaili Muslims. The Aga Khan's concern with the cultural dimension of development, in addition to the experience gained through the Aga Khan Award for Architecture, led to the establishment, in 1988, of the Aga Khan Trust for Culture, which now incorporates the Award. The Trust's two other major areas of activity are the Education and Culture Programme and the Historic Cities Support Programme. The Aga Khan Trust for Culture forms part of the Aga Khan Development Network, a group of private international development agencies created by the Aga Khan. The Network represents a contemporary endeavour of the Ismaili *Imamat* to realize the social conscience of Islam through institutional action. Philosophically, the Network is grounded in Islam's ethics of inclusiveness, compassion, sharing, self-reliance, respect for health and life, the cultivation of a sound and enlightened mind, and humankind's collective responsibility for sustainable physical, social and cultural environments. Network agencies have mandates that range from the fields of health, education and rural development to the enhancement of non-governmental organizations and the promotion of private-sector enterprise. They are currently working to improve living conditions and opportunities in countries on four continents.

THE AGA KHAN AWARD FOR ARCHITECTURE

Of all the major architectural prizes, the Aga Khan Award for Architecture is perhaps the only one that, in addition to celebrating the finest fruit that embellishes the tree of Architecture, encourages the roots that nurture the plant. These dual concerns place the Award in a truly unique position; for in order to make its selections, the Award must of necessity be concerned not only with product but also with process and the issues that generate that process. Thus, since its inception almost twenty-five years ago, the Aga Khan Award has been an extraordinarily inventive and courageous enterprise, seeking always to understand the fundamental issues of the societies it addresses and to identify those subtle but pivotal watersheds that shift our perspective and open up a world of new possibilities.

In Islamic societies, these issues and possibilities are even more diverse than we might imagine. For most of us Islamic architecture conjures up the incredible beauty of the Alhambra and the Taj Mahal, of Isfahan and Fathepur-Sikri, as well as unforgettable images of closely packed habitats, ranging from the kasbahs in Algiers and Fez to the hill towns of Yemen. In short, an urbane oasis architecture, with impervious walls to keep out the hot, dry desert winds, built of timeless materials – mud, brick and stone. And this set of conditions stays surprisingly constant in a long geographic belt that runs all the way from Casablanca in the west to Delhi in the east. But the truth is that the vast majority of Muslims lives even further away than Delhi – in fact, most of them live east of Calcutta. What they have to deal with is not the hot, dry climate of the desert, where the air can be trapped in courtyards and humidified, but the hot, humid conditions of South-East Asia, where the air must constantly be kept moving, and light porous walls and cross-ventilation are essential. Furthermore, most of them live not in urban centres but in rural areas, so they need an architecture that is concerned with rural typologies and not urban ones.

The present set of Awards for the 2001 cycle articulates all these issues very eloquently. Not only do the projects demonstrate a wide and pluralistic range, from low-income housing in India to an elegant new hotel in Malaysia, but, more than in any previous cycle, there is a real emphasis on rural habitat. The considerable efforts of the last twenty-five years are beginning to show results. There is a growing awareness in the rest of the world that the Aga Khan Award for Architecture probably represents the most serious process of all the major architectural awards. And from that, the people of the Islamic world have garnered a new sense of confidence in their own judgment and architectural skills.

This cycle also includes a special event, one that has occurred only twice before in the history of the prize – the presentation of a Chairman's Award. In 1980 this was awarded to the great Egyptian architect Hassan Fathy, and in 1986 to Rifat Chadirji of Iraq. In this cycle the Chairman's Award is presented to the extraordinarily brilliant and original genius, Geoffrey Bawa of Sri Lanka. There could have been no better choice. For five long decades Bawa has always marched to the beat of his own drum, creating an incomparable body of work that we can all now enjoy. In presenting him with the Award, we honour not only the great sensitivity of his world, the power and inventiveness of the language he has created, and the exquisite beauty of the fruit he has harvested but also the vital importance of the roots he has nourished all these years.

FOREWORD
CHARLES CORREA

The Aga Khan Award for Architecture

MODERNIZATION AND LOCAL CULTURE

–

–

–

–

THE EIGHTH CYCLE OF THE AGA KHAN AWARD
KENNETH FRAMPTON

Introduction

Furthermore, outsiders cannot 'assume away' the local cultural milieu. It exists. Any outside assessment of a notable building will be 'read' by the milieu and the assessment itself will become a vector for change, in one way or another, that acts upon the milieu. This is particularly true of the attitudes of Western observers, who represent the dominant culture of the world today, vis-à-vis Muslim intellectual elites who seek to redefine their identity in non-Western terms in the face of a historical break in Muslim cultural continuity…

The manifestations of the cultural situation also include another significant front: the advancing insertion of a modern, rapidly changing technology into everyday lives traditionally governed by other concerns. The suitability of the technology, its adaptation to the needs of the population and the societal context, is only one part of the issue. This is the part that has usually concerned architectural critics when looking at buildings. For both building as a process and building as a product, the technology issue has invariably been addressed in terms of suitability and adaptation. In more sophisticated analyses, the intrusion of technology into aesthetic precepts and norms has also been addressed. But the present discussion would add that technology, with its various facets and dimensions, involves a rationalist ordered universe, whose frame of reference is governed by a reductionist logic. That in turn confronts a manifest reality of semantic disorder due to the disintegration of semiotic frameworks referred to above. This confrontation is resolved when the rationalistic logic is used to provide new conditions that elicit a new set of cultural symbols, much as the Modern Movement in international (Western and Japanese) architecture came into being, thus liberating and broadening the horizons of an authentic yet contemporary cultural response within the Muslim world.

Ismaïl Serageldin

'The Search for Excellence in Muslim Societies', 1986.[1]

Ever since John Turner's pioneering work with squatter settlements in Latin America, documented in his 'Dwelling Resources in South America' of 1963,[2] and since Hassan Fathy's *Architecture for the Poor*, first published in English in 1973,[3] we have been only too aware of the overwhelming scale of global poverty, and the limits of architecture as a bourgeois practice when confronted with the degree zero of human habitation. Whether we like it or not, we are returned to these grass-roots circumstances by the Master Jury of the eighth cycle of the Aga Khan Award for Architecture. For four of the nine works premiated in this cycle focus once again, as in the past, on the all but unbridgeable gulf that separates the deprived millions of the late-modern world – those whom Frantz Fanon once called the 'wretched of the earth'[4] – from those of us who, by talent or by chance, find ourselves momentarily carried on the wave of global prosperity.

As Serageldin remarks elsewhere, much of the built environment in the Muslim world is in fact dependent on non-architects. For this reason alone the Aga Khan Trust for Culture finds itself simultaneously patronizing the art of architecture with a capital A, while still acknowledging the harsh realities of a world that desperately needs its assistance at many levels, not least of which is the triennial disbursement of the Award. Fifteen of the seventy-eight projects selected by Award Master Juries between 1980 and 1998 were, in fact, largely devoted to housing schemes for those living at the low end of the economic spectrum in the Islamic World.

The Award's distribution for other categories over the same period may be gleaned from the following record: some 53 per cent were given to architecture and urban design, 22 per cent to conservation, 5 per cent to landscape and 20 per cent to housing. A comparable breakdown for this year's cycle works out somewhat differently, with three awards going to architecture, one each to the categories of conservation and landscape, and the four remaining awards being dedicated, if not to housing exactly, then certainly to the amelioration of the environment for the benefit of the rural poor.

The marked absence of conservation works in the current cycle of the Award is in strong contrast to the pattern of premiated projects in all previous cycles. Is this shortfall due to an absolute decline in the number of recent conservation projects in Islamic countries, or is it that our standards with regard to conservation have become so strict as to preclude works that would have passed muster some years ago? The New Life for Old Structures programme, representing this category in the current cycle, deserves to be warmly endorsed not only for its preservation of old houses and bathhouses in Isfahan, Yazd, Zanjan, Tabriz and Boushehr, as well as thirty ongoing programmes in twenty-one other cities, but also for the social outreach of the new uses

Kenneth Frampton

accommodated in this stock. Irrespective of how this programme may eventually be evaluated in terms of restorative technique versus social relevance, the restoration of the historical fabric of Iran's cities is not an inconsequential achievement, even if it seems to pale before some of the astonishing realizations premiated in the past, such as the rehabilitation of Old Sana'a in Yemen and the restoration of the centre of Bukhara in Uzbekistan, both being recipients in 1995; the reuse of the Rüstem Pasa Caravanserai in Edirne, Turkey, a recipient in 1980; and the controversial but exquisite refurbishing of the Azem Palace in Damascus, premiated in 1983.

Would we be justified in seeing the apparent decline in the scope and scale of conservation as indicative of a fundamental shift in our mode of evaluation? Have our standards become so exacting that they inhibit a more liberal approach to the reconstitution and appropriation of antique form? These are questions that patently go beyond the boundaries of the Award, for the world as a whole seems to be increasingly caught in the progressive bureaucratization of conservation. We are ever more frequently presented with a zero-sum game, with archaeological purity on one side of the argument and crass reconstructivism operating with impunity on the other, the latter leading to a kind of Disney World that nobody needs or desires. Between these two poles there surely exists an intelligent, sensitively calibrated middle ground, as the British architect David Chipperfield and his restoration consultant Julian Harrap are demonstrating in their proposals for restoring the Neues Museum in Berlin.[5]

Symptomatic of emerging bureaucratic rigidity is the fact that most of the architecture of Carlo Scarpa would be unrealizable today if it were subject to the strictures imposed by the average Italian *soprainten-denza*.[6] While for Scarpa restoration always involved an act of reconstitution, he nonetheless invariably displayed a certain discretion towards the antique fabric in which most of his works were situated. However, the liberties that he occasionally took in reifying one particular historical moment rather than another would no doubt be regarded as anathema today by the puritans of conservation. Does a similar restraint account for the fact that among the seven restoration works shortlisted for this cycle, only the restoration of a number of Safavid and Qajar structures could be regarded as being sufficiently faithful to the original? Or is it that

the secondary cultural status of a house or a bathhouse is such that they may be more freely modified to suit a new use, whereas a historical monument of higher stature must be preserved as is, in all its ruined Ruskinian purity? We know that Camillo Boito, the Italian nineteenth-century theorist of preservation, advocated a more moderate attitude towards restoration. So when it comes to the current debate over the limits of culturally responsible conservation, we should perhaps return to the pragmatic humanism that underlay many of his arguments.[7]

While such questions are perhaps unanswerable with any specificity, they are certainly worth asking in the context of the Aga Khan Trust for Culture, which has long since taken the lead in helping to preserve the cultural traces of the Muslim world in physical form. First, via the Award programme itself, through recognizing the urgency of conserving Islamic heritage irrespective of whether it is a singular monument or an extensive piece of urban fabric. Second, through the Historic Cities Support Programme dedicated to reconstituting remote cultural markers or revitalizing decaying urban fabric as the embodiment of a unique way of life. In the first instance I have in mind the 1996 restoration of the Baltit Fort in the Karakoram Mountains in Northern

Pakistan, while a telling example of the second surely resides in its recent efforts to conserve and revitalize the historical Stone Town of Zanzibar. The measured restoration and adaptation of historical buildings in Iran has, needless to say, its own intrinsic merit, particularly when, as is the case here, the reutilization of such structures yields public facilities of various kinds, capable of enriching the cultural and economic life of their immediate context.

Among the numerous settlements nominated for this cycle, none perhaps is more directly representative of the interaction between modernization and local culture than the rehabilitation of the village of Aït Iktel in Morocco. The overall income of this remote community is complemented by migrant workers sending back a portion of their wages, and it was just this Berber diaspora that was galvanized into action by a local anthropologist, Dr Ali Amahan, with the founding of the Association Aït Iktel de Développement. Two external factors stemming directly from the modernization process had a decisive impact on the formation of this organization: first, the closing of certain factories in France in the 1980s, where a number of Berber immigrant workers had been formerly employed; and second, the continuous drought induced in the High Atlas Mountains by changes in the global climate, which compelled village women to walk further and further to obtain water. Lest we conceive modernization solely as a recent side effect of globalized First-World consumerism, we might note that the local climate had already been rendered more arid by the wholesale deforestation of the mountains throughout the nineteenth century. The insatiable demand of the poor for firewood and construction lumber led to the ravaging of the local forests, at a rate of

New Life for Old Structures, Iran.

Aït Iktel, Abadou, Morocco.

Modernization and Local Culture

depletion that, happily, has seen a significant reduction over the last decade.

Apart from affording access to basic education and providing itself with street lighting for the first time in its existence, Aït Iktel seems to have attained a significant improvement in its native culture, even if its basic housing stock remains essentially unaltered. Electrification and the provision of a reliable water supply has virtually eliminated the burden traditionally placed upon women, and Aït Iktel has reduced its illiteracy rate to 75 per cent as opposed to the national average of 81 per cent. All of this is even more impressive when one realizes that the average village income per capita is US$ 90 per annum, as opposed to the national minimum wage of US$ 140 per month.

Clearly there is little here that may be subsumed under architecture in the professional sense, and indeed this degree-zero building culture seems to be as removed from the more sophisticated cultures documented in Bernard Rudolfsky's *Architecture Without Architects* of 1969 [8] as it is from the contemporary constructional norms of the developed world. This is perhaps what may be intended by the term local culture as opposed to the vernacular in a stylistic sense of the term. For here the vernacular, such as it is, can be seen as undergoing an all but invisible transformation as migrant building workers return home to build their own houses. Needless to say, they bring with them, however simple it may be, an alien building technology. However, even though the standard concrete frame is gradually being more generally adopted, along with the use of rendered block-work, traditional stone walls still hold their own against the seemingly infinite mountain range from which they have been quarried since time immemorial.

Equally removed from anything that we could possibly classify as traditional architectural practice is the work of the so-called Barefoot Architects, local people with no formal education who work at the Barefoot College in India. The college was established in 1972 by the sociologist Bunker Roy as a way of departing from the academic orientation of the Indian social-work tradition by engaging and training ordinary people, so as to cultivate a kind of Deweyesque, self-reliant community. Once again, the process of modernization was the prime mover at more than one level: first, perhaps because the natural aridity of the climate has recently become exacerbated by global warming; and

second, because the first five years of the institution would once again be largely spent in searching for a more reliable source of water and in electrifying some 110 villages in the district of Silora. This technological infrastructure was complemented over the next decade by improving the community's native skills for agricultural and craft production, enabling, in turn, the construction of installations dedicated to the harvesting of rain and the harnessing of solar power. In addition, the Barefoot Architects built a campus for the college. Based on a design that seems to have been arrived at on a collective basis, the architectural result is at once both surprisingly formal and informal. The basic building syntax itself could hardly be more strict and severe, even though the technology employed is quite hybrid, so that it is not something one could possibly recognize as vernacular in the traditional sense.

In the last analysis, the Barefoot College displays all the traits of a Utopian community abstracted from another moment in history. One is irresistibly reminded to an equal degree of both Rabindrannath Tagore's Santiniketan College and of Charles Fourier's paradigm of the *phalanstère*, even if there is no parade ground on which any kind of *phalanx* could possibly assemble. In its stead there is a central theatrical space and open-air stage flanked on its wings by the cultural and collective core of the college, made up of the main dining room, the puppet theatre and administrative offices. A great deal of attention is clearly given to the enrichment of the cultural life of the institution, as is suggested by the presence of smaller stage platforms in the courtyards of the residential blocks. It is difficult to ignore the implicit symbolism of this neo-Kahnian layout, with its main axis of diagonal symmetry bisecting both the rainwater-storage tank and the principal

The Barefoot College campus, Tilonia, India.

Kenneth Frampton

open-air stage. Buckminster Fuller's geodesic domes have been widely employed throughout, not only for the larger volumes but also for emergency shelter, invariably made out of scrap metal by the master craftsman Rafeek Mohammed . These temporary thatched shelters, often sided in mud-brick, recall the intermediate technology of the 1960s, along with the anarchic ethos of Drop City in Arizona and the *ad hoc* 'know-how' that was once commonly available in the pages of *The Whole Earth Catalog*.[9]

Designed by Jafar Tukan and Partners in collaboration with Ralph Montgomery, the SOS Children's Village in Jordan is also a somewhat Utopian development, even if its physical form derives from the standard typology of a decentralized family-based orphanage, as this has evolved under the auspices of SOS Villages International. Here the interface between modernization and the vernacular stems from Jafar Tukan's reinterpretation of the local stone building tradition, achieved through the application of traditional masonry to an *in situ* concrete frame filled with cement-block backing. Once local craftsmen had been trained in this mode of construction, they were able to disseminate the technique fairly widely, although local architects have so far remained relatively indifferent to the regionally expressive dimension of this approach. In addition to the rubble stonework, one should note the sensitive inflections achieved by the placement of concrete lintels and sills over and under the window openings, while the windows themselves are delicately screened, as in the past, by louvred timber shutters. With its solar roof panels and its ultramodern concrete wind towers, the syntax of this settlement, despite its adaptation of the vernacular, largely eschews any overt reference to the Islamic tradition.

Irrespective of the official auspices under which they were realized, the works discussed so far have depended for their success on one or two visionary figures without whom they would never have been realized. The Kahere Eila Poultry Farming School in Koliagbe, Guinea is no exception to this rubric. It is the outcome of an unlikely collaboration between a local veterinarian, Bachir Diallo, and a wealthy Finnish woman, Eila Kivekäs, the school being created as a way of addressing the appalling lack of protein in the average Guinean diet. It was the first of many local initiatives supported by Kivekäs and her development association, Indigo, which eventually led her to settle in Mali town in 1993.

As a result, she commissioned a house for her own occupation, to be designed by the Finnish architects Heikkinen–Komonen. This simple but somewhat mannered house, known as the Villa Eila, was supposed to have been a demonstration of the latent cultural potential of arts and crafts in Guinea. A number of its features, above all the roof and the bamboo sunscreening, do succeed in reflecting some aspects of local building technique, while suggesting the possibility of combining these tropes with modern spatial concepts and conveniences. The overall result, however, has apparently not withstood the ravages of the climate, together with a general lack of maintenance, particularly after Kivekäs' demise in 1999.

The modestly monumental Kahere Eila Poultry Farming School, by the same architects, seems to have fared much better, and in this regard, we might note that its design was based on a more rational plan. The confrontation here between modernization and vernacular culture is oddly provoked by the use of Nordic timber techniques ingeniously employed by the Finnish architects in the

construction of the mono-pitched roofs. In addition, cable-tied timber joists are used for the wider spans covering the central classroom and its monumentally symbolic portico, opening towards the centre of the court. Otherwise, the complex uses local materials. The main body of assembly is built out of 15-by-15-by-30-centimetre hand-pressed blocks made of stabilized earth mixed with a small quantity of cement, while the roof tiles were also made on site along with traditional mats of woven wooden lathes that form the ceilings of the accommodation. All ventilation is natural and passes through the roof and, although the farm is well supplied with water, electricity and sewerage, there is no telephone connection. This affords a dramatic idea of how remote and primitive this institution really is – it stands there implanted like the emblem of a future hybrid civilization in the middle of the bush.

It is hard to imagine a more dramatic icon of global warming than a tropical rainforest, for today we are all hyper-aware of the way in which the lush vegetal cover of the earth's surface is being rapidly depleted. This imparts to the Datai Hotel in Malaysia an ambiguous yet critical character. Ambiguous because its erection has, of necessity, entailed the destruction of a certain amount of forest, including a 30-kilometre autoroute without which the northern part of the island would have remained inaccessible; critical because of the extreme sensitivity with which the construction of the hotel was approached by the architect, Kerry Hill.

While the complex adheres to the local Malay tradition of building on stilts, one can hardly speak of a vernacular here since the structure is extremely mixed. Concrete foundations and a certain number of steel spans are combined with brick walls rendered in plaster, while a considerable amount of timber cut directly from the forest is used for, amongst other things, the voluminous roofs with their large overhanging eaves protecting the verandas of the hotel from the monsoon. Further evidence of the perennial interplay between modernization and local culture is the fact that, although air-conditioning is available, it is treated as an option rather than a necessity.

Despite the fact that this is a hedonistic complex catering to the high end of the elite global market, its built-in environmentalism plays itself out at both an autodidactic and didactic level. It is autodidactic in the sense that, subject to the advice of the engineer,

SOS Children's Village, Aqaba, Jordan.

Kahere Eila Poultry Farming School, Koliagbe, Guinea.

Modernization and Local Culture

Rahulan Zain, and Dr Appanah of the Malaysian Forest Research Institute, both client and architect had to learn how a structure of this dimension could be responsibly inserted into such a delicate environment. It is didactic in the sense that, simply by staying in a rainforest guests receive spontaneous instruction as to the nature of the fauna and flora surrounding them, while the hotel has sponsored a separate field experiment into the relative productivity of agricultural versus forest land.

In his warm appraisal of the building, the eco-tech Malaysian architect Kenneth Yeang writes: 'Who says that a critically regionalist architecture cannot be luxurious, commercial and pleasurable? This incredible hotel on the island of Langkawi, off Penang in Malaysia, is a clever reinterpretation of native architecture as a contemporary resort hotel. It demonstrates simply an approach to hotel architecture that is not Modernist, not pastiche, but innovates in all aspects of rethinking traditional Malay architecture. The architectural excellence of this genre has not been equalled elsewhere.'[10]

Our progressive reaction to the modernization process seems to assume a critically topographic, place-oriented character the closer one moves to the centre of 'universal civilization', to coin Paul Ricoeur's felicitous term.[11] This is surely evident in the compensatory form of the Olbia Social Centre at the Akdeniz Üniversitesi on the outskirts of Antalya. Typologically speaking, the introverted spine of the centre suggests a nineteenth-century galleria. This has both positive and negative connotations. Positive to the extent that the double-sided covered walkway connects to transport facilities, student accommodation and faculty buildings. Negative to the degree that an introspective 'galleria', when not inserted into existing urban fabric, always produces on its outer perimeter an alien 'backstage' space, to which one cannot relate in a meaningful way (see the residential student union designed by Diamond and Myers and built in the campus of the University of Alberta, Edmonton, Canada in 1969). However, Cergiz Bektaş provides a countervailing component to this 'backstage' effect, in an open-air amphitheatre with its *scena* facing into the campus.

The inner spine (galleria) is lined from end to end with cafeterias, restaurants, student clubs, multi-purpose auditoria, galleries and an array of shops. It is just this commercial continuum that enabled the university, with its limited funds, to take advantage of the BOT method (Build, Operate and Transfer), by which private investors glean the profit from the complex for nine years before transferring the ownership back to the university. Does not this ambiguous status – part shopping centre, part student forum – account for the mixed iconography of the syntax employed? Thus, on the one hand, stone-faced, anti-seismic, concrete-framed construction with mono-pitched, red-tiled roofs, having agrarian connotations, while on the other a wide ornamental watercourse, lined on both sides by an all but neoclassical timber pergola carried on pre-cast concrete columns. This combination suggests a

Datai Hotel, Pulau Langkawi, Malaysia.

Top: Olbia Social Centre, Antalya, Turkey.
Bottom: Bagh-e-Ferdowsi, Tehran, Iran.

Kenneth Frampton

promenade through a discrete mall, rather than the traditional dense urban fabric that was the original inspiration. Be that as it may, there seems to be little doubt as to the popular reception of this work or as to its role in compensating for the absent 'space of public appearance' in a late-modern campus.

Landscape features in the awards of the ninth cycle in two coincidentally topographic but otherwise unrelated works. The first, Bagh-e-Ferdowsi in Iran, is an enormous perambulating park that transforms beyond recognition the originally delimited Islamic concept of the garden as an earthly embodiment of paradise. The second, the Nubian Museum in Egypt, was apparently first conceived as issuing from the ground on which it stood, like the ancient, mythic culture it was intended to embody and represent.

The more extensively *paysagiste* of the two is evidently Bagh-e-Ferdowsi in Tehran. Conceived as a complement to the 12-hectare Baghe Sangi Jamshidieh, realized in the 1970s by essentially the same design team, Bagh-e-Ferdowsi is an even more stony, rambling park covering the lower foothills of the Alborz Mountains so as to create a green buffer zone between the burgeoning modernized megalopolis of Tehran and the relatively unmediated wilderness of the mountains. Apart from their differing size and shape, the primary distinction between these two complementary parks is that, where the first park is well served with an ample supply of water, the second is seemingly somewhat dry, even though commendable efforts have been made to provide fountains and water channels running alongside the stone pathways.

There are other differences between the two parks that are possibly indicative of the distinct historical circumstances under which they were created. For whereas the earlier park largely eschewed the importation of exotic, non-native shrubs, the later park seems to have been accorded a more popular, even populist tone through the introduction of large flowering borders or banks. Moreover, where the restaurants and other auxiliary service buildings of Baghe Sangi Jamshidieh were integrated into the landscape in such a way as to be virtually invisible, those of Bagh-e-Ferdowsi, representing the ethnic groups that make up the population of the country, have been treated as iconographic way stations. Hence the Azeri, Kurdish, Turkmen and Zagros houses, originally conceived as cultural institutions, which now function as teahouses mostly under private ownership.

Despite the use of imported stone from the respective regions of Iran, these various attempts to represent local culture in architectonic terms would seem to be largely scenographic. In fact, the way in which masonry has been generally deployed in these two parks could hardly be more different. For where, in the first, case stones are placed so as to suggest some form of natural geological stratification and displacement, in the second, the stones are bonded together in such a homogeneous manner as to arrive at a continuously swirling plasticity, reminiscent of the zoomorphic forms of Antonio Gaudi's Park Güell in Barcelona. Bagh-e-Ferdowsi is most impressive at a broader, panoramic scale, where the paved mountain roads undulate through the landscape as though they were fragments of a regionally scaled, fortified wall.

Finally realized in 1997, the Nubian Museum at Aswan, Egypt, exists as a consequence of modernization in the most direct sense imaginable. Had not a vast section of the Nile Valley been totally inundated in 1971 to provide hydro-power for the new High Dam at Aswan, thereby creating Lake Nasser, there would have been no need to house the priceless remains of the twenty-two Egyptian monuments covered by the man-made flood.

Dr Mahmoud El-Hakim originally conceived the building as an internal topography, served by pedestrian ramps, surrounding a large statue of Rameses II in the centre, lit from above. The statue still occupies this position, although the elimination of the ramps and the skylight from the scheme means that it is now neither readily visible nor naturally illuminated. El-Hakim had intended that the flow of objects and visitors would culminate at the lowest level of the museum, at its eastern portico, where it would divulge into an external exhibition court. According to the landscape architects, Werkmeister and Heimer, this sequence was then to have been amplified by a stepped rock formation conducting visitors back onto the roof of the building, from which a stream of water would have descended as a metaphor for the Nile. Subsequent modification of El-Hakim's design weakened the didactic and cultural intentions of the initial concept, despite successful remedial efforts on the part of Dr Leila Masri to rescue something of Werkmeister's original landscape.

From the point of view of the never-ending conflict between modernization and cultural form, the initial brief seems to have been compromised by the modern cura-

torial tendency to maximize air-conditioning and artificial illumination, often at the expense of the relationship between users and exhibits. However, the building is well detailed and well constructed, its architecture seems successfully to represent the rich legacy of Nubian culture, and it asserts itself on the site in such an authoritative manner as to counter the popular prejudice that Nubia is a backward part of the country.

I have elected to view the works premiated for the eighth cycle of the Award as responses, at distinctly different cultural levels, to the impact of modernization. This seems to be the one factor linking architecture with a capital A as we find, say, in the Nubian Museum, to what we might more generally characterize as local environmental culture, as this appears in the Aït Iktel development, the work of the Barefoot Architects, the SOS Children's Village and the Kahere Eila Poultry Farming School. In each of these instances, the common denominator seems to have been a concerted effort to improve local living standards in the face of largely indifferent forms of modernization, operating at a globalized distance at ever-increasing speeds. What would appear to be intrinsically Islamic about all these works is the assumption of responsibility for the basic well-being of the society on the part of a relatively small number of enlightened individuals.

However, with the exception of the Jordanian orphanage, we can hardly speak of architecture in professional terms in these four projects, particularly with regard to sites as remote as the plains of Rajasthan, the High Atlas Mountains and the interior of Guinea, where the societies in question have been confronted with the challenge of improving the conditions of everyday survival and the maintenance of health. This goal has been achieved in part by revitalizing traditional forms of habitation and construction

Nubian Museum, Aswan, Egypt.

Modernization and Local Culture

pertinent to the region and its climate, and in part by providing new water, power and sewerage infrastructures through sustainable forms of eco-technology. This, in turn, has led to additional benefits at the socio-cultural level, particularly with regard to the emancipation and education of women and, in the case of the Barefoot Architects, with respect to the categorical repudiation of the persistent legacy of the Indian caste system.

These four realizations, all of which display an ecological dimension in one way or another, serve to remind us of the way in which building culture, broadly understood, is ultimately inseparable from culture as such, in both a political and an artistic sense. It is a sign of the times that, as with the Olbia Social Centre, all four works were achieved without any significant input on the part of the state – at either a local or a national level – as opposed to those premiated works realized in Iran, Egypt and Malaysia. In these other, possibly more professional, undertakings either the local government or the nation state played a key role in initiating the project. Under this sponsorship, architecture tends to assume a more broadly instrumental character, subtly linked, even in the case of Iran, to pressures deriving from modernization and to the processes of cultural disruption and displacement: for example, the obsolescence, from a universal middle-class standpoint, of the traditional Iranian courtyard house, not to mention the brutal autoroute incisions cut into the traditional labyrinthine urban fabric as long ago as the early 1930s. No doubt, the impact of modernization in the case of the Datai Hotel takes a somewhat different form, although even here, the indisputable quality of its eco-sensitive, quasi-vernacular architecture has ultimately been achieved in the name of exotic tourism, devised, all but exclusively, for the entertain-

ment and enjoyment of a global, jet-setting elite. In sum we are still some way from the authentic contemporary cultural response to which Serageldin aspires.

By way of an exemplary response in this regard we may invoke the Chairman's Award of the eighth cycle, given in honour of the distinguished Sri Lankan architect Geoffrey Bawa. Bawa's work has always reflected in the most subtle way this tension between modernization and local culture, never more categorically, perhaps, than in his civic buildings, culminating in the new Sri Lankan Parliament building opened on an artificial lake in Kotte near Colombo in 1982. It is hard to think of any contemporary legislative building that so seamlessly integrates a rational approach to both plan and structure with traditional tropes, as expressed in the hierarchical gradation of the trabeated frame from concrete to timber to fine-grained wooden grillwork. This gradation, combined with delicately profiled copper roofs rising over a concatenation of pavilions, ends in a work of breathtaking nobility, from which there emanates a sense of expansive benevolence. At the risk of exaggerating, one may perhaps claim that, whereas Bawa's plans were invariably orthogonal and hence both modern and efficient, particularly when combined with precisely trabeated structures, his details and, above all, his low-pitched tiled roofs, embodied much of the Sri Lankan building tradition, almost as an untouched continuum, as valid now as in the past.

Except perhaps for his persistently rational planning, this double condition tends to become totally fused in his domestic work. This is at once evident in the Ena de Silva House, built early in his career in 1960, and in his own house, realized in its entirety some eight years later. Both of these houses are in fact interstitial courtyard complexes, as are most of Bawa's subsequent houses in one way or another. As such, they are an integral part of his prowess as a designer of gardens, a practice that, for him, is inseparable from that of architecture. This proto-ecological green dimension surely attains its apotheosis in the 25-acre Lunuganga garden that Bawa has worked on continuously for the past half century, as a demonstration of that which he once ironically called 'action gardening'. In this singular, infinite work, one senses, once again, that feeling for tranquillity and labyrinthine beauty that somehow lies momentarily suspended beyond such abstract categories as modernization and its other.

Notes

1 Ismaïl Serageldin, 'The Search for Excellence in Muslim Societies', in *Space For Freedom* (Aga Khan Award for Architecture, 1986) p 62.

2 John Turner, 'Dwelling Resources in South America' in *Architectural Design*, August 1963, pp 360–93. See also by the same author *Freedom to Build* (New York, Macmillian, 1972).

3 Hassan Fathy, *Architecture for the Poor: an experiment in rural Egypt* (Chicago University Press, 1973).

4 Frantz Fanon, *Les Damnés de la terre* (Paris, F Maspero, 1961).

5 Accepting that there is no absolute answer to the dilemma posed by restoration, this team has assumed a synthetic approach to restoring, stabilizing and simulating the original form of the Neues Museum. To this end Chipperfield and Harrap have developed a computerized representation of a series of alternate levels to which the ruined interior might be restored.

6 See Ellen Soroka, 'Restauro in Venezia' in *Journal of Architectural Education*, May 1994, pp 224–41. Soroka quotes Scarpa to the effect that: 'By *restauro* (restoration) is not meant only to repair old buildings; our duty is rather to give them a new lease of life so that we may be able to live today and tomorrow…In architecture all the existing buildings form a part of the *matière*.'

7 Camillo Boito, *Questioni pratiche di belle arti* (Milano, 1893). In a similar vein, Viollet-le-Duc argued in his *Dictionnaire raisonée de l'architecture française* (1854–68) that, while empathizing with the architect of the original buildings, the restorer must remain open to different methods of restoration.

8 Bernard Rudolfsky, *Architecture Without Architects, a short introduction to non-pedigreed architecture* (New York, Museum of Modern Art, 1969).

9 *The Whole Earth Catalog* (Menlo Park, California, Portola Institute Inc, 1969). Influenced by Buckminster Fuller's techno-anarchic views as to the need to develop proto-ecological, synergetic systems on a world scale, this catalogue contains self-help survival information in almost every conceivable field, from simple shelter construction to hydroponics and the exploitation of solar energy.

10 Kenneth Yeang, quoted in the Aga Khan Award for Architecture 2001 Technical Review Reports.

11 Paul Ricoeur, 'Universal Civilization and National Cultures', 1961 in *History and Truth* (Evanston, North West University Press, 1965).

Geoffrey Bawa: Ena de Silva House, Colombo, 1960.

Kenneth Frampton

GENIUS OF THE PLACE: THE BUILDINGS AND LAND- SCAPES OF GEOFFREY BAWA

-

—

DAVID ROBSON

Chairman's Award

Consult the Genius of the Place in all;
That tells the Waters or to rise, or fall;

Epistle IV to Richard Boyle, Earl of Burlington,
'Of the Use of Riches'
Alexander Pope

In 1998, when Geoffrey Bawa suffered a massive stroke that left him paralyzed and unable to speak, it seemed that every vital part of this extraordinary man had been extinguished. But friends soon discovered that he had survived, trapped inside his wasted body, and found ways to reach him. Three years later his condition has barely improved, but he is now at least able to make regular visits to his beloved garden at Lunuganga, some 60 kilometres south of Colombo. There, each morning, he meets with Michael and Arsha, the two young architects who look after his estate, and together they plan the cutting and pruning to be undertaken during the day. Michael points towards the surrounding clumps of trees, Arsha whispers in his ear and Bawa gestures with his good left hand. Only someone who has witnessed this strangely moving charade could credit that the Bawa confined deep within his corporeal prison is still in touch with the garden he has been fashioning for more than fifty years.

Bawa's final internment could be seen as a cruel parody of his earlier existence. He has always been a very private person, whose life was divided into clearly defined chapters, whose friends were kept in separate compartments, whose inner thoughts and feelings were seldom, if ever, exposed, and whose deeply held architectural beliefs were carefully camouflaged. When asked to explain his buildings he would usually offer witty ripostes or banal homilies and pretend to hold no truck with theorizing. And yet, over a period of forty years, Bawa succeeded in establishing a canon of revolutionary architectural prototypes for his native Sri Lanka. In the context of a newly independent country emerging from four centuries of colonial hegemony he forged a new architectural identity that drew together the different strands of a complex ethnic weave and exploited a rich history. As the Malaysian architect Kenneth Yeang has said: 'For many of us Asian architects Geoffrey Bawa will always have a special place in our hearts and minds. He is our first hero and guru.'[1]

Bawa was born in 1919 in what was then the British Crown Colony of Ceylon. On a map of the world Sri Lanka appears to be a peripheral place on the very edge of the Asian land mass, cut off from centres of power and major trade routes. Its history has been marked, however, both by its proximity to India and by its strategic position in the Indian Ocean between the Arabian Sea and the Bay of Bengal. India was the source of Sri Lanka's early settlers and of its two main religions, Buddhism and Hinduism, while the ocean brought seafarers from Arabia and China. During the twentieth century, Sri Lanka's population increased almost sixfold and today it stands at about twenty million. Nearly three-quarters of this total are Sinhalese, who are mainly Buddhist; about one-fifth are Tamils, predominantly Hindu; and the balance is made up of Moors or Muslims – the mixed descendants of Arab seafarers – and smaller groups of Malays, Chetties, Dutch Burghers and Eurasians.

Geoffrey Bawa and Ulrik Plesner at the Shell Bungalow, Anuradhapura, 1960.

David Robson

Bawa's own family history reflects much of this ethnic and cultural diversity. His grandfather, Amaduwa Bawa, was a Muslim lawyer from the ancient Arab port of Beruwela, who went to London to further his studies and married a Miss Georgina Ablett of Islington. Their son, Benjamin, became one of the most successful lawyers of his generation, and in 1908 married Bertha Schrader, the daughter of a Dutch Burgher called Frederick Justus Schrader and his Scottish–Sinhalese wife. Benjamin Bawa died in 1923 and Geoffrey, who was only four years old at the time, was henceforth brought up by his mother and two maiden aunts.

In 1938 Bawa went to Cambridge to read English. He later studied law in London and, after qualifying, returned to Ceylon at the beginning of 1946 and worked for a Colombo law firm. He soon tired of the legal profession, however, and set off on two years of travel that took him through the Far East, across the United States and eventually to Italy, where he decided to buy a villa overlooking Lake Garda. But the plan to buy an Italian villa fell through and, as Ceylon was slipping out of the British Empire, Bawa returned home and bought a derelict rubber estate at Lunuganga. Here his interest in landscape and architecture was kindled. Making the transition from restless traveller and reluctant lawyer to builder and gardener, Bawa set out on the serendipitous journey that made him independent Sri Lanka's most prolific and influential architect.

The garden project fired Bawa's imagination but laid bare his lack of technical knowledge and in 1951 he embarked on a trial apprenticeship with H H Reid, the sole surviving partner of the British colonial practice

Edwards, Reid and Begg, founded in Colombo in 1923. When Reid died suddenly a year later, Bawa returned to England and joined the third year at the Architectural Association in London. He was the oldest student in the school and is remembered with affection for his striking appearance, his Rolls Royce and his argumentative debates with tutors. Finally qualifying in 1957 at the age of thirty-eight, he returned to Ceylon and became a partner of Jimmy Nilgiria, a Parsee architect who had taken over Edwards, Reid and Begg after Reid's death.

Working first with a young Danish architect, Ulrik Plesner, and then with the Tamil engineer K Poologasundram, Bawa gathered around himself a group of designers drawn from every corner of Ceylon's ethnic maze. In addition to his immediate office colleagues this group included the artist Laki Senanayake, the designer Barbara Sansoni, and the batik artist Ena de Silva, all of whose work figures prominently in Bawa's buildings. After Jimmy Nilgiria's retirement in 1967, Bawa and Poologasundram continued to practice under the title 'Edwards, Reid and Begg' for the next twenty years.

Bawa's early work included office buildings, factories and schools, influenced by the 'Tropical Modernism' of Maxwell Fry and Jane Drew and ultimately Le Corbusier. The classroom block he designed for Bishops College in Colombo in 1960 is typical. Another key typology was the private house. For more than a century, Sri Lankan domestic architecture had been dominated by British models, and traditional courtyard forms had been largely ignored and forgotten. The typical British 'bungalow' was a cellular villa, extrovert in concept, which occupied the centre

of a large garden plot. However, the population of Sri Lanka was exploding and Colombo was rapidly being transformed from a leafy Garden City into a modern Asian metropolis. Land prices were rising and plot sizes shrinking, exposing the bungalow type's limitations in providing privacy and ventilation. Bawa instinctively grasped the problem and set out to find a solution.

In his first houses, built at the end of the 1950s, he deconstructed the colonial bungalow and rearranged its constituent parts to create semi-enclosed spaces. There followed a series of 'frame houses' – designed with Plesner and inspired in part by Scandinavian models – in which an orthogonal concrete frame was infilled to incorporate covered terraces, garden courts and planted roof gardens. Initially Bawa's commitment to Modernism drew him to white abstract forms and horizontal roof lines, but he was soon forced to admit that overhanging roofs offered necessary protection against tropical sun and rain.

His first breakthrough came with a house for a doctor, A S H de Silva, built in 1959 on a steeply sloping site in Galle, on the south-west coast of Sri Lanka. Here the deconstructed elements were reassembled on an exploding pinwheel plan and held together by a single raking roof plane. But although the various linked pavilions created enclosed and half-enclosed garden courts, the house remained relatively extrovert and the gardens reached out towards the surrounding landscape.

Bawa's next client was Ena de Silva, the daughter of a Kandyan aristocrat and wife of the Inspector General of Police. She had bought a small corner plot in the Colombo

suburb of Cinnamon Gardens and wanted a house that would be modern and open but embody features of the traditional manor houses she had known as a child. After interviewing several architects she turned to Bawa, whom she had initially rejected because of his dilettante image: 'I had seen him driving around in his Rolls with his scarf blowing in the wind and didn't like the look of him.'[2] In fact the two became close friends, and Bawa later recalled: 'I remember talking to Ena, seeing her surrounded by all the things she liked – all she wanted was brick walls and a roof. The plan came about largely because she, and consequently I, wanted a private compound that would not be overlooked by neighbours.'[3]

Bawa's solution employed the same elements as the Galle house but he now carved them out of a solid form. The result is a totally introspective house that emphasizes void as much as solid and allows a free flow of space from inside to outside. The plan consists of a chequerboard arrangement of linked pavilions and small courts, all disposed around a large central court, or *meda midula*, and contained within a limiting perimeter wall. The overpowering presence of the tiled roof and the generally localized palette of materials give this house a vernacular feel, and yet the highly articulated and open plan is totally modern in its effect. Space flows continuously from inside to outside and long vistas range across a series of indoor and outdoor 'rooms' to create the illusion of infinite space on what is a relatively small plot.

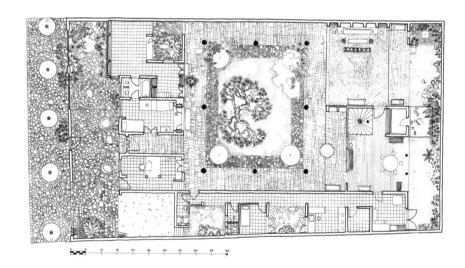

Top left: Entrance to the A S H de Silva House, Galle, 1959.
Top right: Central court and living room of the A S H de Silva House.

Bottom: Ground-floor plan of the Ena de Silva House, Colombo, 1960.

David Robson

Geoffrey Bawa
View through the living room to
the main court of the Ena de
Silva House.

022

Geoffrey Bawa
Main court, Ena de Silva House.

024

Geoffrey Bawa
View from a guest room across to the
living room, Ena da Silva House.

025

Geoffrey Bawa
Staircase, Ena de Silva House.

026

Geoffrey Bawa
Tiled roof, Ena de Silva House.

A further strand in the private house typology is exemplified by the Polontalawa Estate Bungalow, built in 1964 for a Swiss plantation company on a remote coconut estate in the Dry Zone. Bawa and Plesner insisted that the client accompany them on a site visit and then persuaded him to build the bungalow in an area of huge boulders, with roofs spanning from rock to rock: 'We discovered a spot full of boulders and we all said how excellent and splendid it would be to build a house there. So we got sticks and string, brought some chairs and sandwiches and set the house out with the contractor, who followed every gesture of our hands.'[4] Growing out of the landscape, the house belongs to a long Sri Lankan tradition of cave temples insinuated between boulders and tucked under cliffs. It employs materials gathered from its immediate surroundings and celebrates the roof as a totally autonomous element.

Contradicting the assertion that Bawa built only for Colombo's elite, in 1966 he designed and constructed a farm school for orphan girls at Yahapath Endera on a rubber and coconut estate near Hanwella, about 30

kilometres east of Colombo. Its buildings were simple and cheap, constructed from locally available materials, including coconut and rubber timber, clay tiles and coconut thatch. Although he placed them on a formal orthogonal grid, Bawa allowed the buildings to 'run with the contours' in section. Individual buildings were positioned carefully to define open spaces and axes and to regulate vistas. Anura Ratnavibushena, who worked on the project, has described how Bawa generated many of his ideas whilst actually on site, developing them in the evening in sketch sections, usually drawn in biro on squared paper. Although no models were made, Bawa was able to visualize the three-dimensional complexities of the evolving design. Ratnavibushena would then work the ideas up into more finished drawings, which would form the starting point for another round of discussions and sketches.

In 1969 Bawa completed the Bentota Beach Hotel – the first purpose-built resort hotel in Sri Lanka and the standard against which all subsequent hotels would be measured. While offering subtle hints of a lost world of ancient palaces, medieval manor houses and colonial villas, it pandered to the needs of the modern tourist, playing on the senses to create a unique and unforgettable experience. Bawa located the hotel at the neck of a spit separating the Bentota River from the Indian Ocean, and raised it on a mound, which he encased in a rubble podium. Its apparent simplicity belies its spatial complexity and the subtleties of its section. In plan it recalls Le Corbusier's design for the Monastery of La Tourette: the main reception spaces at the summit form an enfilade of rooms around a square courtyard, above which two floors of bedrooms

Top left: Living room, Polontalawa Bungalow, Dry Zone, 1964.
Top right: Dormitory, Yahapath Endera Farm School, Hanwella, 1966.

Centre: Wash-house, Yahapath Endera.
Bottom: Drawing of the approach to Yahapath Endera.

seem to float, with their balconies facing out towards the sea. From these balconies guests experience the tropical landscape beyond the confines of the hotel – the thunder of the ocean, flashes of sunlight on the swaying palm fronds, the shriek of a peacock, the orange glow of the setting sun as it slips below the horizon. But when they quit their rooms they are confronted by the civilized landscape of the courtyard below, where they smell the spices of the evening meal and hear the chink of glasses and the babble of foreign tongues.

Even when the hotel was new its materials – rough granite, polished concrete, terracotta, dark-stained timber, handloom – gave it a well-worn and lived-in feel, as if it were a building that had been discovered rather than designed. Conceived during a period when building materials were in short supply, it was built entirely by local contractors. Only thirty drawings were produced and many of

the details were worked out on site by Bawa with the craftsmen. Almost all of the furniture was designed in the office and made locally, and the rooms were filled with art works by Bawa's friends.

The 1970 elections brought in a left-wing coalition government and heralded a period of economic restraint and uncertainty in Sri Lanka. Suddenly Bawa felt uneasy about his future and even contemplated emigrating. He starting looking for work abroad and in 1971 opened an office in Madras on the strength of a commission to extend the Connemara Hotel. This led to a number of other projects, including the design of a staff club in a suburb of Madurai. During this period Bawa also converted a sugar factory on the island of Mauritius into a weekend retreat and designed a group of villas at Batujimbar on the southern tip of Bali. Prospects soon improved on the home front, however, and the new government turned to

Top left: Aerial view, Bentota Beach Hotel, southern Sri Lanka, 1969
Top right: View across the pool at the Bentota Beach Hotel.

Bottom left: Interior, Pallakelle Factory Unit, near Kandy, 1970.
Bottom right: Exterior, State Mortgage Bank, Colombo, 1976.

David Robson

Bawa for a number of public projects that challenged him to address the problem of the workplace in a tropical environment. These included an estate of simple but effective hipped-roofed factory units at Pallakelle near Kandy and a delightful office building for the Agrarian Research and Training Institute in Colombo.

A further project of this kind was the 1976 design for the State Mortgage Bank, described at the time by Kenneth Yeang as 'probably the best example of a bioclimatically responsive tall building to be found anywhere in the world'.[5] The restricted site for this twelve-storey high-rise, wedged between Colombo's Hyde Park Corner and the southern tip of the Beira Lake, lies across the road from Bawa's childhood home. Its lozenge-shaped plan creates a profile that changes dramatically according to viewpoint, appearing slender towards the junction and much flatter towards the park and the lake. It is capped by a floating concrete canopy that reveals the geometric logic of the concrete structure below.

The 1977 elections returned to power a United National Party government committed to re-establishing a free-market economy. As part of a massive wave of development projects, President Jayawardene asked Bawa to prepare designs for a new Parliament building at Kotte, about 8 kilometres east of Colombo. Bawa was given a totally free hand, with the proviso that the project had to be completed in time for an official opening in 1982. Poologasundram took charge of the management of the programme and at his

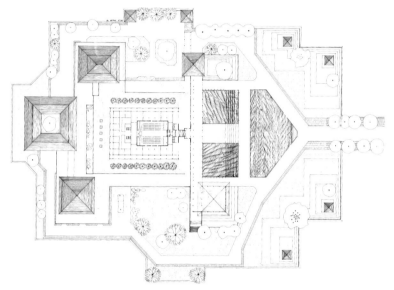

suggestion the construction project was contracted to the Japanese firm Mitsui. A special team of architects was established under Vasantha Jacobsen, Bawa's main assistant, eventually producing over five thousand drawings – a far cry from the days of the Bentota Beach Hotel.

Bawa proposed that the marshy valley of the Diyavanna Oya be flooded to create a vast lake and that the new capitol be built on a knoll of high ground, which would become an island at the lake's centre. Its cascade of copper roofs would be seen floating above the new lake from the approach road at a distance of 2 kilometres. The design places the main chamber in a central pavilion surrounded by a cluster of five satellite pavilions, each defined by its own umbrella copper roof and seeming to grow out of its

own plinth, although the plinths are actually connected to form a continuous ground and first floor. The main pavilion is symmetrical about the debating chamber but the axiality is diffused by the asymmetrical arrangement of the lesser pavilions around it. As a result, the pavilions each retain a separate identity but unite in a single upward sweep of tent-like roofs that make abstract reference to traditional Kandyan roof structures.

The new Parliament opened in April 1982 against a background of growing communal tension. Its commemoration stone recorded ironically that the architects were 'Edwards, Reid and Begg' adding, almost as an afterthought, the names of Geoffrey Bawa, Dr K Poologasundram and Vasantha Jacobsen – a Burgher-Moor, a Jaffna Tamil and a Sinhalese Buddhist.

Bottom left: Debating chamber,
National Parliament, Kotte, 1982.

Top: Aerial view, National
Parliament.
Centre: Plan, National Parliament.

029

Genius of the Place

Geoffrey Bawa
Exterior views of the University of
Ruhunu, southern Sri Lanka, 1984.

031

Geoffrey Bawa
Exterior and entrance, Kandalama
Hotel, near Sigiriya, 1991.

During the 1980s Bawa worked on designs for the new University of Ruhunu near the southernmost tip of Sri Lanka. The magnificent site straddles two hills, giving views across a lake towards the southern ocean. Comprising 50,000 square metres of buildings to accommodate 4,000 students, it was built by Dutch contractors and took eight years to complete. Bawa's design deploys over fifty separate pavilions linked by a system of covered loggias on a pre-dominantly orthogonal grid, using a limited vocabulary of forms and materials borrowed from the Porto-Sinhalese traditions of the late medieval period. At the same time it exploits the changing topography of the site to create an ever-varying sequence of courts and verandas, vistas and clos-ures. The result is a modern campus, vast in size but human in scale.

The projects of the early 1980s brought Bawa international recognition and his work was celebrated in a Mimar book by Brian Brace Taylor in 1986 and in a London exhibi-tion. But the Parliament building and Ruhunu had left him exhausted. He missed the direct control he had exercised over his earlier pro-jects and spent less and less time in the office in Alfred House Road. His partner, Poologasundram, had been offended by Bawa's failure to acknowledge him in the book or exhibition and the two grew apart. After 1989 the practice effectively ceased to function. Bawa was now in his seventies and it was widely assumed that he would retire to Lunuganga and contemplate his garden. Nothing, however, could have been further from the truth. The closing of the office signalled a new period of creativity, and he began to work from his Bagatelle Road home with a small group of young architects to produce a steady stream of fresh designs.

By now Bawa's fame had spread far beyond the shores of Serendib and he received many requests to lend his name to projects in the Far East. He and his young colleagues embarked on a series of ambi-tious designs: a massive extension to the Hyatt Hotel on Bali; a tropical glasshouse in Singapore; a huge villa hotel on the island of Bintan in Indonesia; a high-rise development in Penang. Requests for private houses also flooded in and Bawa produced sketches for clients in Ahmedabad, Delhi, Bangalore and Singapore. None of these projects came to fruition, however, and Bawa treated them as test beds for new ideas, to be used when the opportunity presented itself.

Such an opportunity arose at the end of 1991 when Bawa was commissioned to design a hotel at the foot of King Kasyapa's rock citadel at Sigiriya in the Dry Zone. True to form, he rejected the proposed site and persuaded the clients to locate the hotel some fifteen kilometres to the south, on a rocky outcrop above the ancient Kandalama tank. The site was virtually inaccessible and Bawa had to be carried to it on an improvised palanquin.

In its final design the 160-bedroom hotel is wrapped around two sides of the rock, with rooms facing across the tank towards Sigiriya and Dambulla. The two wings are connected by a cavernous corridor running through the rock from the hotel entrance to the main reception areas. Bawa's use of a starkly expressed concrete frame and a flat roof is ideally suited to the location, and the hotel seems to grow out of its site in a simi-lar way to the earlier house at Polontalawa. The frame supports a second skin of timber sunbreakers, which in turn carries a screen of vegetation, while the flat roof has been transformed into a fantastic tropical garden.

Aerial view. Kandalama Hotel.

Lounge, Kandalama Hotel.

David Robson

The tectonic form allows the hotel to hug the shape of the ridge, so that its open-sided corridors run alongside the cliff face. In the public areas, the materials used complement the large expanses of naked rock to convey a wholly appropriate feeling of austerity.

Three houses from this period reveal the distance an artist travels in order, it would seem, to come full circle. Built at the bottom of the owners' former garden in Colombo, the de Soysa House of 1990 is a minimalist tower of concrete and glass jostling between a clump of trees. The Jayakody House of 1993 creates a civilized retreat on an awkward Colombo site, ascending from an almost subterranean world of shady courtyards

to a rooftop pool terrace that looks out across the surrounding roofscape. In contrast, the Jayawardene House of 1997 is a weekend retreat on the red cliffs of Mirissa overlooking the sweep of Weligama Bay. Here the visitor climbs a narrow track from the busy main road and, after a final twist, discovers a breathtaking view across the bay framed by a grove of swaying coconut palms. These hide a platoon of black columns and a thin horizontal roof – a simple pleasure pavilion on a stepped plinth facing towards the ocean and the setting sun. Forty years

separate these houses from the doctor's house in Galle, and yet they reveal the same concern with distillation and simplicity.

Left: Exterior, de Soysa House, Colombo, 1990.

Top: Cross-section, Kandalama Hotel. Centre: Exterior, Jayakody House, Colombo, 1993.

Above: Views of the Jayawardene House, Mirissa, 1997.

Genius of the Place

034

Geoffrey Bawa
Interior and veranda, de Soysa House.

Geoffrey Bawa
Interiors, Jayakody House.

Bawa's last two hotels were executed with the sure touch of a master. The Lighthouse Hotel of 1995 defies the southern ocean from a rocky promontory on the outskirts of the old Arab port of Galle. The sea is inhospitable – huge breakers roll in incessantly from the Indian Ocean – but the views are stunning. The strategy is both to confront the relentless crashing of the waves and to provide contrasting areas of shelter and tranquillity. The lower slopes of the rock are encased in rubble retaining walls, housing the main entrance and services. A massive *porte cochère* leads past the reception desk to a vertical drum enclosing the main stair, which spirals upwards among a swirling

mass of Dutch and Sinhalese warriors sculpted by Bawa's old friend Laki Senanayake. The lounges and restaurants carry memories of old rest houses and planters' clubs, while the furnishing of the terraces and verandas is solid and rugged to withstand monsoons. No single space is self-contained or complete: each is in part the consequence of a previous space and the anticipation of a subsequent one; each retains links with its neighbours and with the outside so that the eye is continually invited to explore the possibilities the building offers.

South of Colombo, the Blue Water Hotel at Wadduwa – one of the last projects that Bawa supervised before his final illness –

Top left and right: Exterior view and main swimming pool, Lighthouse Hotel, Galle, 1995.

Bottom left and right: Staircase, with figures by Laki Senanayake, and terrace, Lighthouse Hotel.

David Robson

sits in an uninspiring coconut grove between a railway line and a long flat beach. The design is a reworking of a traditional rest house, blown up to a massive scale with long axes and vast courtyards to create a minimalist palace, a perfect setting for ceremonies and celebrations.

Bawa's health had been deteriorating for some time before he suffered his final stroke in early 1998. At the time he was still involved with a number of projects and work on these continued under the direction of his associate Channa Daswatte. Two of the projects, the Spencer House in Colombo and the Jacobsen House in Tangalle, have since been completed to their original designs, while a third in Mumbai is still on site. In 1997 Bawa's design for a new Presidential Secretariat was approved by the President, but during the following year the site was changed and the project is now being carried forward by Daswatte in the spirit of the original design.

Looking back over Bawa's career, two projects seem to hold the key to an understanding of his work: the garden at Lunuganga and his own house in Colombo. Both have been many years in the making and both have served as laboratories for new ideas. The town house is a haven of peace, locked away from the busy and increasingly hostile city, an infinite garden of the mind constructed like a puzzle on a tiny urban plot. In contrast the estate at Lunuganga is a distant retreat, an outpost on the edge of the known world, which challenges the infinite horizon of the ocean to the west and the endless switchback of hills to the east, reducing a vast open landscape to a controlled series of outdoor rooms, a civilized garden within the larger garden of Sri Lanka.

The Colombo house is an essay in architectural synthesis. In 1958 Bawa bought the third in a row of four small bungalows in a short cul-de-sac at the end of a narrow suburban lane and converted it into a *pied-à-terre* with a living room, bedroom, tiny kitchen and room for a servant. When the fourth bungalow became vacant it was colonized to serve as a dining room and second living room. Ten years later the other two bungalows were acquired and integrated into the composition, the first being demolished to make way for a four-storey structure incorporating a library and roof terrace, and the second becoming a guest wing and later the 'home office'.

Over the last forty years the house has been subject to constant change and the

identities of the original bungalows are now all but lost. The final result is an introspective labyrinth of rooms and garden courts that together create the illusion of infinite space. Words like inside and outside lose all meaning: here are rooms without roofs and roofs without walls, all connected by a complex matrix of axes and internal

vistas. If the main part of the house is an evocation of a lost world of verandas and courtyards, the tower rising above the carport is nothing less than a reworking of Le Corbusier's Maison Citrohan, serving as a periscope as it rises from a shady netherworld to give views out across the treetops towards the sea.

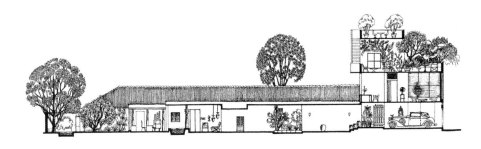

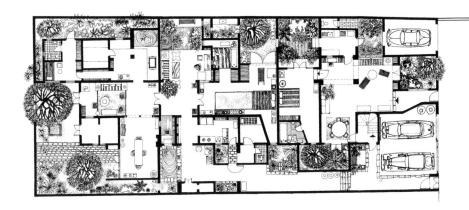

Top left and right: View from the entrance and central seating area of Geoffrey Bawa's house in Colombo, 1958-68.

Centre and bottom: Cross-section and plan, Geoffrey Bawa's house.

038

Geoffrey Bawa
Views of the main pavilion,
Jayawardene House.

039

Geoffrey Bawa
Exterior and interior of the Blue
Water Hotel, Wadduwa, 1997.

The garden at Lunuganga sits astride two low hills on a promontory jutting into a brackish lagoon off the Bentota River. In 1948 there was nothing here but an undistinguished bungalow surrounded by 25 acres of rubber trees. Since then hills have been moved, terraces cut, woods replanted and new vistas opened, but the original bungalow survives within a cocoon of added verandas, courtyards and loggias. Looking south from the main entrance terrace, a corridor of trees frames a view of a large urn in the middle distance marking the summit of Cinnamon Hill and pointing to a distant Buddhist temple. The area to the east of the bungalow has been transformed into a series of interconnected terraces stepping down towards the lake's edge and framed by a guest house, an office pavilion and a sculpture gallery. To the north a lawn runs from the foot of a spreading aralia tree towards the undulating parapet of a steep cliff, offering views across a water meadow towards the lake.

This is a civilized wilderness, not a garden of flowers and fountains; it is a composition in monochrome, green on green, an ever-changing play of light and shade, a succession of hidden surprises and sudden vistas, a landscape of memories and ideas. Works of art are carefully placed to form objects for contemplation, punctuation marks on routes, pointers or distant beacons: a leopard lies in the dappled shade beside the lake, guarding the water gate; a young boy beckons on the edge of the cliff; a grotesque Pan grins up from the edge of the paddy.

Lunuganga seems to be so natural, so established, that it is hard to appreciate just how much effort has gone into its creation. Hardly a year has passed since 1948 without some new element being added, some new area being colonized. The various buildings constructed over the years appear simply to have grown out of the ground, carefully restored remnants of some earlier period of occupation, messages on a palimpsest. Nor is it apparent how much work is needed to maintain such careful casualness. Ignore the garden for a week and the paths and staircases will clog up with leaves; after a month the lawns will run wild; in a year the terraces will start to crumble; and in two or three years the jungle will return.

After the passage of more than fifty monsoons Sri Lanka has lost its innocence and Bawa has grown old. As he sits in his wheelchair on the terrace and watches the sun setting across the lake it may be that he reflects on his achievements. Perhaps the garden had simply been waiting for him to discover it beneath a canopy of jungle? But this is a work of art, not of nature: it is the contrivance of a single mind and a hundred pairs of hands, working with nature to produce something 'supernatural'.

Plan, Lunuganga Estate, Southern Sri Lanka, 1948-present.

David Robson

041

Geoffrey Bawa
The Broad Walk, Lunuganga.

042

Geoffrey Bawa
Path, Lunuganga.

042
Geoffrey Bawa
Rice paddy and lake, Lunuganga.

044

Geoffrey Bawa
View from the main terrace,
Lunuganda.

Geoffrey Bawa
the sculpture gallery, Lunuganga

Notes
1 Kenneth Yeang, quoted by Michael Keniger in *Bawa: Recent Projects 1987–95* (Brisbane, Queensland Chapter of the RAIA, 1996).
2 Ena de Silva in conversation with the author.
3 Geoffrey Bawa in conversation with Channa Daswatte.
4 Geoffrey Bawa in conversation with Channa Daswatte.
5 Kenneth Yeang, quoted by Michael Keniger in *Bawa: Recent Projects,* op cit.
6 Geoffrey Bawa, ' Ceylon, a Philosophy for Building' in *Architects' Journal,* 15 October 1969.

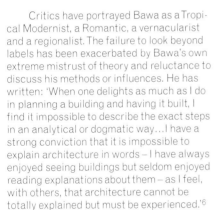

Critics have portrayed Bawa as a Tropical Modernist, a Romantic, a vernacularist and a regionalist. The failure to look beyond labels has been exacerbated by Bawa's own extreme mistrust of theory and reluctance to discuss his methods or influences. He has written: 'When one delights as much as I do in planning a building and having it built, I find it impossible to describe the exact steps in an analytical or dogmatic way…I have a strong conviction that it is impossible to explain architecture in words – I have always enjoyed seeing buildings but seldom enjoyed reading explanations about them – as I feel, with others, that architecture cannot be totally explained but must be experienced.'[6]

It is difficult to pin down Bawa's influences. He himself has spoken of English country houses, Italian gardens, the Alhambra in Granada, the forts of Rajasthan and the Keralan Palace of Padmanabhapuram, and has acknowledged his debts to Sinhalese classical and vernacular architecture. But

he has also been influenced by the twin heroes of the Modern Movement, Mies van der Rohe and Le Corbusier, whose work resounds through what at first sight seem to be Bawa's most traditional pieces.

Bawa's work should be viewed in the context of a country whose population has almost tripled since independence and whose communities have been fractured by bitter political and ethnic disputes. In today's Sri Lanka, fast cars vie with bullock carts on the narrow roads, young girls in saris sew jeans for Marks & Spencer, and farmers gather in the evening under the village tree to watch the latest American soap on *rupavaheeni* – 'the picture from heaven'. Although it might be thought that his buildings have had no direct impact on the lives of ordinary people, Bawa has exerted a defining influence on the emerging architecture of independent Sri Lanka. In celebrating the island's rich history and cultural diversity he has developed a new architectural language, truly of its place.

Top left and right: The office pavilion and sitting room, Lunuganga.

Bottom left and right: Views of the guest house, Lunuganga.

Genius of the Place

BIBLIOGRAPHY

Bawa, Geoffrey, 'Ceylon, a Philosophy for Building' in *Architects' Journal*, 15 October 1969.

Bawa, Geoffrey and Plesner, Ulrik, 'Ceylon – Seven New Buildings' in *Architectural Review*, February 1966.

Bawa, Geoffrey; Bon, Christoph and Sansoni, Dominic, *Lunuganga* (Singapore, Times Editions, 1990).

Beng, Tan Hock, *Tropical Retreats* (Singapore, Page One, 1996).

Brawne, Michael, 'The Work of Geoffrey Bawa' in *Architectural Review*, April 1978.

Brawne, Michael, 'The University of Ruhuna' in *Architectural Review*, November 1986.

Brawne, Michael, *From Idea to Building* (London, Butterworth Heinemann, 1992).

Brawne, Michael, 'Paradise Found' in *Architectural Review*, December 1995.

Bryant, Lynne, 'House in Colombo Sri Lanka' in *Architectural Review*, May 1983.

Daswatte, Channa, 'Bawa on Bawa' in Meng, Tan Kok, *Asian Architects 2* (Singapore, Select Publishing, 2001).

Hill, Kerry, 'The Pleasure of Architecture' in *Monument* no 16, 1996.

Jayawardene, Shanti, 'Bawa – A Contribution to Cultural Regeneration' in *Mimar* no 19, January–March 1986.

Keniger, Michael, *Bawa: Recent Projects 1987–95* (Brisbane, Queensland Chapter of the RAIA, 1996).

Khan, Hasan-Uddin, *Contemporary Asian Architects* (Cologne, Taschen, 1995).

Killick, John, 'The Decaying Neighbourhood' in *Architectural Design*, October 1956.

Lewcock, Ronald; Özkan, Suha and Robson, David, 'Bawa' in *Arredemento Dekorasyon*, June 1992.

Nakamura, Toshio, 'The Architecture of Geoffrey Bawa' in *Architecture & Urbanism (A+U)* no 141, June 1982.

Plesner, Ulrik, 'Polontalawa House' in *Arkitektur (DK)* no 3, 1969.

Plesner, Ulrik, 'Buildings are for People' in *Arkitektur (DK)* no 3, 1971.

Powell, Robert and Meili, Marcel, 'Special Edition: The House' in *Architecture & Urbanism (A+U)* no 314, November 1996.

Powell, Robert, *The Tropical Asian House* (Singapore, Select Books, 1996).

Powell, Robert, *The Urban Asian House* (Singapore, Select Books, 1998).

Richards, J M, 'Ceylon Pavilion at Expo 70' in *Architectural Review*, August 1970.

Richards, Sir James, 'Geoffrey Bawa' in *Mimar* no 19, January–March, 1986.

Robson, David, 'An Island Parliament' in *Caravan 4*, 2000.

Robson, David and Daswatte, Channa, 'Serendib Serendipity: The Architecture of Geoffrey Bawa' in *AA Files* no 35, May 1998.

Scott, Rupert, 'Two Bawa' in *Architectural Review*, May 1983.

Taylor, Brian Brace, *Mimar Houses* (Singapore: Concept Media, 1987).

Taylor, Brian Brace, 'Club Villa, Bentota' in *Mimar* no 24, June 1987.

Taylor, Brian Brace, *Geoffrey Bawa* (Singapore, Concept Media, 1986, and London, Thames & Hudson, 1995).

Yoos, Jenifer et al, 'Special Edition: The House' in *Architecture & Urbanism (A+U)* no 338, November 1998.

Geoffrey Bawa at Lunuganga in 1990.

David Robson

RECIPIENTS OF THE 2001 AWARD

\-

\-

\-

\-

The Aga Khan Award for Architecture

1 New Life for Old Structures, Various locations, Iran
2 Aït Iktel, Abadou, Morocco
3 Barefoot Architects, Tilonia, India
4 Kahere Eila Poultry Farming School, Koliagbe, Guinea
5 Nubian Museum, Aswan, Egypt
6 SOS Children's Village, Aqaba, Jordan
7 Olbia Social Centre, Antalya, Turkey
8 Bagh-e-Ferdowsi, Tehran, Iran
9 Datai Hotel, Pulau Langkawi, Malaysia

Location of Award Recipients

The nine members of the Master Jury for the 2001 Aga Khan Award for Architecture met twice to select the winners from the 427 projects presented. Of these, thirty-five were reviewed on site by a team of sixteen distinguished experts, whose presentations brought the many complex aspects of each project to the Jury's attention.

A key concern of the jury as it pursued its deliberations was with architecture dedicated to enhancing conditions of life within diverse communities and groups in Muslim societies. Issues of environmental sustainability, social equality, cultural and historical identity and human dignity also informed the Jury's decisions.

Some of the projects are organized to encourage disadvantaged communities to advance their conditions by increasing productivity, improving their built environment and sharing access to modern culture and communication. Joint efforts by people who benefit from the modern economy and those who have remained in rural conditions have made it possible to reverse the constant flow of migration with the concomitant depletion of local human resources and deterioration of environmental and living conditions. Some projects respond to educational needs, such as preserving the life and culture of an ancient civilization, while others provide instruction in techniques of animal production to enrich diet and nutrition.

The Jury also considered the positive role of tourism in modern economies in the context of architecture that respects the environment and introduces local culture within the built work. Projects that secure the future of superb historical buildings within towns and that create new parks for urban communities also represent important inclusions in the Jury's decisions. Public, industrial and religious buildings, as well as conservation projects, were also considered, but none met the standard expected of this Award.

New Life for Old Structures, Various locations, Iran
Aït Iktel, Abadou, Morocco
Barefoot Architects, Tilonia, India
Kahere Eila Poultry Farming School, Koliagbe, Guinea
Nubian Museum, Aswan, Egypt
SOS Children's Village, Aqaba, Jordan
Olbia Social Centre, Antalya, Turkey
Bagh-e-Ferdowsi, Tehran, Iran
Datai Hotel, Pulau Langkawi, Malaysia

STATEMENT OF THE AWARD MASTER JURY

The 2001 Award Recipients

The Aga Khan Award for Architecture

NEW LIFE FOR OLD STRUCTURES

—

—

—

—

VARIOUS LOCATIONS, IRAN

This project has received an Award for helping to promote sustainable urban regeneration by rescuing structures from deterioration and demolition. In a number of successful interventions in several historical Iranian cities, the programme has attempted to preserve the country's unique built heritage through the adaptive reuse of private and public spaces. It has created a new way to address the social needs of contemporary society in historical urban areas, providing economically viable solutions that meet the needs of younger generations.

Five Iranian cities have benefited from a bold government programme to refocus attention from development on their outskirts towards the reuse of architecturally unique buildings in their historical centres. In a context of widespread deprivation and rapid population growth, a number of key projects have launched a process of urban regeneration by illustrating the potential of restored buildings to meet current needs in a commercially viable way. This has inspired private investors to undertake parallel projects for the reuse of historical houses and a number of guest-house developments. The overall effect has served to rescue significant traditional building typologies – particularly the courtyard house – from the threat of demolition, while both improving local living conditions and raising awareness in the community about retaining the historical urban fabric. At the same time, the projects have demonstrated Iran's rich cultural heritage and provided opportunities for the employment and training of craftsmen in a range of traditional construction skills.

Between the significant public buildings that survive in the cities of Isfahan, Yazd, Zanjan, Tabriz and Boushehr, the historical centres comprise a dense built fabric,

primarily of mud or fired brick, arranged over one or two storeys. Circulation around the neighbourhoods is through complex networks of narrow streets and pedestrian alleys, some of which have houses built over them. One architecturally notable feature of traditional houses is that, because of their arrangement around internal courtyards, the street façade is of little decorative significance. The articulation and adornment of interior elevations and decoration of the surrounding rooms are in great contrast to the understatement of the exterior, however.

A recent move away from use of the internal courtyard as the focus of domestic life has given rise to the construction of homes, often on more than two floors, which directly overlook the narrow streets or alleys. Along with the general neglect of traditional homes, which are often perceived to be inappropriate for contemporary domestic needs, unregulated development poses a very real risk to the historical fabric. It was to address this threat that a programme was established by the Ministry of Housing and Urban Development in 1988 to arrest the physical and social decline of the city centres through restoration and reuse of historical buildings. Buildings are acquired, restored and sold or

The programme aims to reuse historical buildings to meet the needs of a fast-growing urban population in Iran. The Khan Bathhouse in Yazd was transformed into a restaurant.

New Life for Old Structures

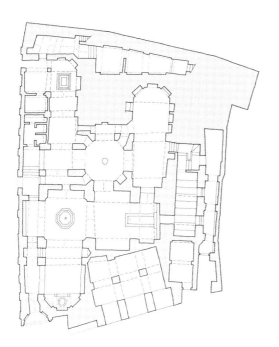

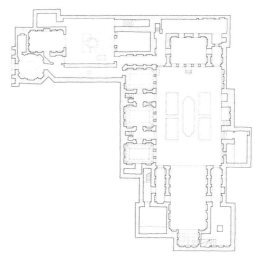

rented to new owners or tenants. An important part of this process has been to identify practical new uses for the restored buildings that are of benefit to the community.

The work is undertaken by the Ministry of Housing's Urban Development and Revitalization Corporation (UDRC), which since 1997 has operated as a corporation, with 51 per cent private investment. In addition to the projects in Isfahan, Yazd, Zanjan, Tabriz and Boushehr, the UDRC has over thirty urban revitalization and development projects ongoing in twenty-one cities. All work related to historical buildings is carried out in close collaboration with the Iranian Cultural Heritage Organization (ICHO) of the Ministry of Culture and Islamic Guidance, which is responsible for identifying, registering and maintaining or restoring significant building complexes and historical structures.

The buildings have been converted, some with great imagination, to accommodate a wide variety of public facilities, which contribute to local social services and the cultural life of the inhabitants. Among the most imaginative reuse examples in Isfahan

has been the transformation of the Vazir Bathhouse, dating from the Safavid period, which has been restored and converted into the Centre for the Intellectual Development of Children and Young Adults. Occupying a site close to the bazaar, the *hammam*, or bath-house, is entered via steps that descend to a series of domed and vaulted spaces. Within the massive structure, some of the dividing walls have been removed to provide continuity of circulation. A dado of traditional blue glazed tiles runs throughout the building to create a robust, colourful and child-friendly environment, adapting traditional finishes to new needs. The high vault of the original dressing room, or *bineh*, is used as a library, while the adjacent steam room, or *garmkhaneh*, serves as a play and reading area. The more intimate spaces that originally housed pools, or *khazineh*, provide the backdrop for art lessons; three of the former pools have been retained and adapted for use as displays. Quarry tiles have been laid with glazed tile inserts in patterns that enable the children to play games, and traditional small glass skylights in the domes

Bottom: A decorated platform for devotional use in a Qajar-period religious structure, now used as an art centre.

Top: Plans of a bathhouse and a traditional courtyard house, typologies threatened by modern development that have proved to be particularly suitable to adaptive reuse.

New Life for Old Structures

provide natural lighting. A ramp, traditionally used to lead animals to draw water from the well, has been ingeniously transformed into a small auditorium.

Other examples of inventive adaptive reuse in Isfahan include the conversion of one of the city's oldest houses into a religious seminary, of a house dating from the Qajar period into a school, and of two further Qajar houses into guest houses. In Yazd, a bath-house has been transformed into a popular restaurant, a fine Qajar religious structure has become a community arts centre and a Qajar residence is now used as the Yazd office of the UDRC. Four residential buildings in Tabriz now house Sahand University's School of Art and Architecture; the Tofighi House in Zanjan has been turned into a Martyrs' Museum and Memorial; and in Boushehr, a port on the Persian Gulf, a Qajar period house has become the Research Centre for Boushehr Studies.

Many of these projects contain a number of unusual architectural features or spatial aspects that have been inventively adapted for contemporary activities. Modern services, including electrical cabling, heating systems and piped water, have been discreetly introduced to all the restored buildings. Structural changes have been kept to a minimum and traditional materials and skills have been used as far as possible, combining them,

where appropriate, with modern materials or methods. This reflects the pragmatic approach adopted by the regeneration scheme as a whole, which aims to make available usable and cost-effective space rather than undertaking meticulous restoration for its own sake. Because the buildings employ long-established traditional features – wind funnels, semi-subterranean spaces, courtyards, timber screens and alabaster glazing panels – they are ideally suited to the climate and also illustrate the effectiveness of these forms for contemporary needs. At the same time, the partial assimilation of the modern construction vernacular ensures that the adaptation process is replicable, affordable and practicable for the future.

A market-driven approach to regeneration is crucial in order to ensure long-term sustainability and the programme has exploited the low cost of centrally located property in comparison to that of outlying areas to reduce costs. The increasing number of projects that have benefited from the urban regeneration scheme has brought new life to the urban centres of Iranian cities, improving living conditions, revitalizing the architectural character, renewing appreciation of the rich cultural heritage, and stimulating awareness in the private sector of just how much investment in a country's delicate historical fabric can benefit everyone.

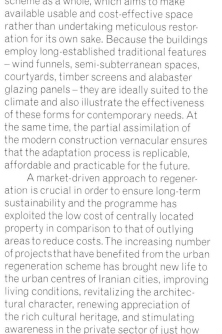

Planners/Conservators
Urban Development and Revitalization Corporation — Hamidreza Sepehri, Director; Ministry of Housing and Urban Development — Serajeldin Kazerouni, former Minister: Iranian Cultural Heritage Organization.

Restoration Architects
S Benesslo, Fariborz Djabarnia, Ghadiri, Nassim Jaafari, Asghar Jeddi, Mohammadreza Khoshfakari, Nikbakht, Mohammadreza Olia', Mohsen Olia', Hassan Ravanfar, F Tehrani, and M H Vaafi.

Project Managers
S Behzadian, P Jamhiri, Hooshang Kianpour, A Moineddini, and Akbar Taghizadeh.

Master Craftsmen
A Ghaffari, H Kamali, Ebrahim Massoudi, A R Ra'iyati, Hooshang Rassam, Hassan Riahi, H Razavi, M Karami, and Abbas Zare' Sharif.

Design   1990—ongoing
Construction 1990—ongoing
Occupancy   1992—ongoing

Tabib House, Boushehr (1993)
Reuse programme   Research Centre for
                  Boushehr Studies

Vazir Bathhouse, Isfahan (1993)
Reuse programme   Centre for the
                  Intellectual Devel-
                  opment of Children
                  and Young Adults

Qodsieh House, Isfahan (1993)
Reuse programme   Religious Seminary

Mojtahedzadeh House, Isfahan (1992)
Reuse programme   Middle School

Nilforoushan House, Isfahan (1998)
Reuse programme   Guest house

A'alam Va'ez House, Isfahan (2001)
Reuse programme   Guest house

Four Qajar residences, Tabriz (1995)
Reuse programme   School of Art and
                  Architecture

Khan Bathhouse, Yazd (1997)
Reuse programme   Restaurant

Moayed A'layi House, Yazd (1997)
Reuse programme   UDRC Offices

Hosayniyeh Nazem ot-Tojar, Yazd (2000)
Reuse programme   Art Centre

Tofighi House, Zanjan (1994)
Reuse programme   Martyrs' Museum

Particular attention was paid to courtyards, which provide protection against hot winds and introduce cooling water and shading plants, as at the Qodsieh House in Isfahan.

ولادت ام المصائب حضرت زینب کبری مبارک باد

057

New Life for Old Structures: The
Hosayniyeh Nazem ot-Tojar is now used
for art and drama classes.

New Life for Old Structures: Restored
decorations at the A'alam Va'ez House
in Isfahan, now a guest house.

059

New Life for Old Structures: The
Vazir Bathhouse in Isfahan, now a
children's development centre.

New Life for Old Structures: [Above left] The Mojtahedzadeh House in Isfahan, now used as a school.

[Above right] An elaborate painted decoration from the Qodsieh House in Isfahan.

[Right] A restored niche with *muqarnas* decoration at the Qodsieh House.

New Life for Old Structures:
[Left] The restaurant interior of the
Khan Bathhouse in Yazd.

[Above left] A library at the
Hosanynieh Nazem ot-Tojar.

[Above right] The Moayed A'layi House
in Yazd, now the offices of the UDRC.

064

New Life for Old Structures: The
Nilforoushan House in Isfahan is a
showcase of restoration skills.

AÏT IKTEL

ABADOU, MOROCCO

The project has received an Award because it exemplifies a new approach to development, environmental conservation and the improvement of living conditions for rural populations. The success of the project was based on mobilizing the experience of emigrant villagers who joined with those who remained in order to change their own destiny. Old buildings have been restored; a water-supply network, electricity and education facilities have been installed; and cooperation between the villagers has enhanced daily life. The project is an example for the entire region, bringing hope to rural communities throughout the Islamic world.

The story of Aït Iktel village, set in the remote High Atlas Mountains, has been described as a 'modern fairy tale'. It is a project in which clients, users and community are one and the same. It demonstrates how a rural community can improve its condition by dedication from within, how people who have left their village in search of employment can continue working with or contribute to the efforts of those who remain, and how, through architecture, a village can be mobilized to improve its present and safeguard its future.

Like many of Morocco's thirty thousand villages, Aït Iktel, located 100 kilometres north-west of Marrakech, existed in relative seclusion until recent years. The village had no electricity and the widespread drought that has plagued the region for the last two decades forced local women to spend many hours each day fetching and carrying water from faraway sources. The national government has only recently begun to address the problems faced by rural areas by encouraging communities and private enterprise to invest in improving conditions.

Most of the residents of Aït Iktel are members of the Ghoujdama Berber tribe and have a history of self-government. Until 1933,

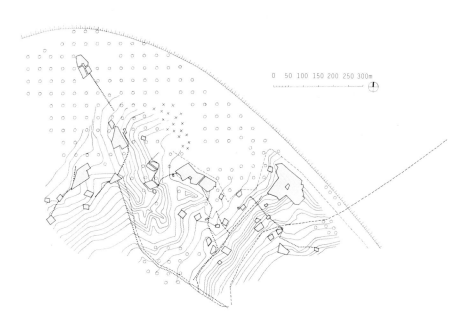

0 50 100 150 200 250 300m

Top left: One of Aït Iktel's three clusters of accommodation. Through the participation of the inhabitants, conditions in the remote village have been vastly improved.

Top right: At the highest point of the village a well and pump room supply water to street fountains in each of the clusters.

Bottom: A plan of Aït Iktel showing the water-supply system and the electricity network that has brought electricity to the area for the first time.

Aït Iktel

no outside administration exercised control over the region, and tribesmen relied on themselves rather than on any formal authority. The village's two thousand inhabitants have traditionally depended on agriculture, mostly grain crops, as the source of income. With antiquated methods, such as manual harvesting, as well as semi-arid weather conditions and the attendant difficulty of raising cattle, the villagers have survived through the flow of income from relatives who have emigrated. At least one member of each family works in a city in Morocco or abroad, providing the means for everyday subsistence to his family in Aït Iktel.

In 1992 Ali Amahan, a native of Aït Iktel, formed the Association Socio-culturelle des Ghoujdama, bringing together members of the tribe who had moved to Casablanca and Rabat. Two years later he became a founding member of the Association de Migration et Développement Local (MDL), an association of forty-five rural non-governmental organizations that aimed to combine the efforts of emigrants living abroad with those of Moroccans from rural backgrounds who had moved to cities. Following the Aït Iktel community's request for help in improving access to water, a well and a manual pump were installed in 1994. The population showed organizational skill by their good maintenance of these new installations. Encouraged by the outcome, influential emigrants founded the Association Aït Iktel de Développement (AID) in 1995, and fully involved themselves in the improvement of their village.

The programme's objectives were to provide basic social services and infrastructural facilities – electricity, a water-supply network, access to education and an improved dispensary – and to organize economic activity through the creation of a craft workshop and improvement of the irrigation system, giving the local community control over decisions and resources. An essential ingredient of the programme's success was the involvement of the users in the organization of the projects, which was almost as important as the physical implementations themselves. All projects were undertaken with the participation of the villagers, who took their own investment decisions, financed projects, used their professional skills, supplied land and labour, and managed their assets. The leaders of the AID worked closely with the *jemaâ*, the traditional assembly of heads of families, with each member's opinion considered and debated until a consensus was reached, allowing villagers to perceive projects as their own. The AID also represented the community in securing government endorsement for their projects and in raising funds.

Today, the community of Aït Iktel enjoys, manages and owns a set of facilities made available by projects implemented through the AID. Electricity runs four hours a day, assuring a basic level of comfort, and some families can afford additional solar equipment. Streets are now lit during the evenings. The entire population has access to water through a supply network that pumps water to traditional street fountains at the entrance to each of the village's three clusters of accommodation. A non-formal school has a schedule that permits children to help their families in daily chores. Classes are held in Arabic and French, and importance is also given to teaching the traditional Berber dialect. Liberated from the heavy labour of carrying water, girls and women have access to literacy and the weaving workshop; around 85 per cent of girls between the ages of four and nineteen are in school. An information centre within the school has helped to increase awareness of hygiene, health, nutrition and culture; a new library has been created; and the existing dispensary has been repaired and upgraded into a health centre and provided with an ambulance. Community cattle-raising and sewage-network projects are planned for the future.

All the facilities and new services have been incorporated either into new structures built in local stone or into the existing architecture of the village, characterized by inlaid stonework in a variety of patterns. Cubic in shape, with living spaces organized around a courtyard, houses usually contain all the functions of rural dwellings, such as a corner for ceramic water jars, a mill and a stable, and each room is used for a variety of functions. All restoration and construction work has been based on traditional techniques or on the construction experience gained by the village's returned emigrants.

Perhaps the most visible and symbolic of the new structures is the 2.5-kilometre-long *seguia*, or canal, which has increased the area of land that can be irrigated. The canal crosses the valley over a bridge constructed in local stone, which has become a landmark in the area. Another important achievement is the construction of two semi-underground reservoirs, which have been sensitively integrated into the natural landscape. The first has a capacity of 105 cubic metres, while a second reservoir, with a

Bottom: A new school faced with
local stonework using traditional
knowledge to preserve the local
architectural character.

capacity of 430 cubic metres, serves other villages in the valley as well as Aït Iktel.

By empowering the community from within, the Aït Iktel Association and the amenities it has created have transformed the local residents into active agents in the improvement of their village life. The facilities they have introduced play an important role in easing the travails of everyday life, especially for women. The AID's accomplish-ments have set a model for surrounding villages, most of which have now created similar community organizations, fostered by Aït Iktel's readiness to share its experi-ence with others. By closing the distance between decision-makers and beneficiaries and circumventing the public sector's shortcomings, the Aït Iktel experience is an exemplary humanitarian endeavour, an inspiration to rural villages around the world.

Project Conception
Ali Amahan

Client
Association Aït Iktel de Développement — Mohamed Amahan, President.

Documentation
Ministère de l'Aménagement du Territoire, de l'Urbanisme, de l'Habitat et l'Environnement — Direction de l'Architecture, Saïd Mouline, Director.

Project History
1994 First well and manual pump installed
1995 Creation of Association Aït Iktel de Développement
1995 First water-supply project
1996 Repair and fitting out of village dispensary
1996 Electrification project commenced
1997 Library installed
1998 Restoration of a house for educational facilities
1999 Irrigation canal built
2000 Second water-supply project

Site area   Approximately 150 hectares
Population   1,849 inhabitants in 122 households
Cost   MAD 2,240,000 (USD 224,000)

Top and bottom: The educational facility in a restored two-storey house provides literacy classes and a weaving workshop that generates income for the village.

Aït Iktel

069

Aït Iktel: The Abadou valley comprises terraced agricultural land and olive plantations.

Aït Iktel: A new irrigation canal has
increased the irrigated area of land
by 26 hectares.

071

Aït Iktel: The canal has made crops
less vulnerable to weather and given
rise to a new cattle-raising project.

Aït Iktel: A bridge was built in
traditional local stone to carry
the canal across the valley.

Aït Iktel: The canal was built in reinforced concrete, using the expertise
of Aït Iktel's emigrant workers.

Aïr Iktel: Water is stored in two
semi-underground tanks, fortuitously
concealed by the uneven landscape.

Aït Iktel: The tanks supply water
not only to Aït Iktel but also to
surrounding villages.

Aït Iktel: One of the three street
fountains that have freed women from
fetching water from faraway sources.

BAREFOOT
ARCHITECTS

TILONIA, INDIA

The Aga Khan Award for Architecture

This programme of works was given an Award for its integration of social, ecological, cultural and educational elements to aid rural development while promoting the architectural traditions of the region. The Barefoot College comprises a unique experiment in employing rural people to implement local social-aid programmes. Its utilization and improvement of the practical construction skills of villagers has led to the creation of buildings that enhance the vernacular tradition of the region and the Barefoot Architects have been able to apply their knowledge in the surrounding community to upgrade rural living conditions.

View of the Barefoot College campus, completed in 1989. The college was founded in 1972 to encourage and advance traditional skills, enabling local people to improve their lives.

The 'Barefoot' philosophy is based on a belief that one hundred years ago village communities thrived with no paper-qualified doctors, engineers, architects or teachers. Such communities developed their own knowledge, which has since been devalued. This belief inspired the foundation of the Barefoot College in 1972 in Tilonia, a small rural community in the arid Indian state of Rajasthan. The college aims to demonstrate that village knowledge, skills and practical wisdom can be used to improve people's lives – an attitude of self-help drawn from Mahatma Gandhi's example. Since rural people already have tried and tested traditions, the college believes that all that is needed is a little training and upgrading, combined with respect for local skills, which are slowly dying out because people are migrating to the cities to look for jobs. The demystification of technology and the dignity of manual labour are crucial lessons of the college.

The founder and present director of the centre, Bunker Roy, wanted to break away from the Indian social-work tradition, which had an urban, middle-class and academic orientation. He envisaged a centre that would attract urban professionals, who would immerse themselves in the realities of rural life and participate in a 'dirty hands',

practical approach as a joint venture between specialists and local residents. Adopting the 'Barefoot approach', a term originally applied to Chinese health workers trained to assist their own rural communities in the 1960s, the Social Work Research Centre (SWRC) began informally on a small scale. The 'Barefoot College', as the centre came to be known, underwent many fundamental changes before achieving its present structure and modus operandi. The current emphasis is on self-reliance for the rural poor; equality across caste, education and gender; collective decision-making; decentralization to support the flow of information and education; and austerity in thought and action.

The college acts as an administrative and training facility, running programmes relating to water supply, community health, education of children, empowerment of women, rural industry and solar technology, among many others. Over the years, the agency has worked with local teachers, health-care workers, solar engineers and handpump mechanics in a comprehensive development plan, implemented with the rural poor and for the rural poor. These programmes have led to the realization of a number of significant buildings embodying the ideals of the college, implemented

Barefoot Architects

by the 'Barefoot Architects' – local members of the college staff. The largest of these projects is a campus for the college, comprising a medical block, library/dining hall, amphitheatre, guest house and residential blocks, craft centre, workshops and workrooms, administrative buildings, and a few other isolated structures, including geodesic domes housing various public facilities. The most diffuse and wide-ranging programme is 'Homes for the Homeless', which has provided over two hundred basic dwellings in surrounding villages. Finally, a rainwater-harvesting system has been developed to harvest rainwater from rooftops – a scheme that has provided scope for community involvement and control over the resource.

The architects found numerous applications in the technology of Buckminster Fuller's geodesic dome. Traditional housing in desert areas has sometimes used wood as a building material, but this has become a scarce resource. Geodesic domes, however, are easily fabricated from scrap metal, which is readily available from disused agricultural implements, tractors, bullock carts and pump sections. The structures are made to a span of 3 metres to house dispensaries, telephone exchanges and other small facilities; 6 metres for small village classrooms and housing; or 10 metres for meeting halls accommodating up to one hundred people. Because of their structural capacities, the domes can be covered with a greater weight of thatch than can traditional small-span structures, reducing the frequency of rethatching. The use of geodesic dome technology also means that expertise now exists in the college for the construction of emergency structures and shelters, including relief housing.

For all the buildings, the college and architects sought to fuse local labour and materials, as an opportunity to advance local skills and practices and to educate workers to adapt new methods to available materials. For example, the creation of geodesic domes from scrap metal was easily taught to a local blacksmith. The success of this approach is exemplified through the construction of the college campus by an illiterate farmer from Tilonia, along with twelve other Barefoot Architects, most of whom have no formal education. They were assisted by several village women, who worked as labourers and carried building materials.

Plans for the Barefoot College campus were drawn and redrawn on the spot and altered several times. A traditional Indian

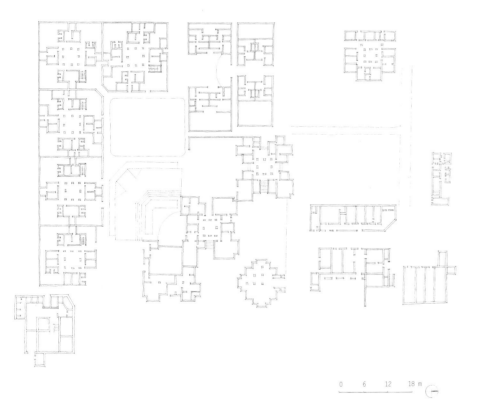

0   6   12   18 m

Top: New technologies are combined with old. Based on a design by Buckminster Fuller, geodesic domes are constructed using scrap metal.

Bottom: The ground-floor plan of the Barefoot College campus. The design of the campus was developed on site by the 'Barefoot Architects' — local people with no formal training.

Project Conception
Barefoot College — Bunker Roy,
Director.

Architects
Barefoot Architects of Tilonia —
Bhanwar Jhat and twelve Barefoot
Architects, construction of the
Barefoot college campus; Rafeek
Mohmmed, Geodesic domes; Laxman
Singh, coordination of the rainwater-
harvesting system; sixty Barefoot
Architects, construction of 200
'Homes for the Homeless'.

Barefoot College
Design   1986
Construction   1986–89
Site area   35,000m²
Built area   2,800m²
Cost   INR 6,000,000
                (USD 21,430)

Rainwater-Harvesting System
(350 installations)
Design   1987
Installation   1988–98
Cost   INR 2 (USD 0.04)
                per litre

Homes for the Homeless
(200 units)
Construction   1986 and ongoing
Cost   INR 600 (USD 20)
                per m²

courtyard format with surrounding verandas was adopted for most of the residential blocks and the main administrative building. The buildings are cubic in form with flat roofs. Local materials, such as rubble stone with lime mortar, were used for load-bearing walls. At ground level the courtyards are highly decorated, as is the custom in Indian vernacular architecture. The college is entirely solar powered and this contributes to its near self-sufficiency in terms of utility services.

The provision of Homes for the Homeless was a natural extension of the college's objective of providing services to the poor. Occupied mainly by farmers and labourers, a typical low-cost flat-roofed house consists of two rooms within a rectangular or L-shaped block, and a water-seal toilet. Walled courtyards around some of the houses offer outdoor space for household activities and chores. Some homes depart from this model and have been altered to suit the basic needs and resources of users. Most of the buildings are constructed from earth-brick, but people with greater economic resources have used other materials, including rubble stone and lime mortar. The houses have proven themselves to be extremely functional and a great improvement on the previous living conditions of their occupants.

Large-scale efforts to provide water in rural areas are typically made by tapping groundwater sources. This process is expensive and short term and often yields brackish water, unfit for human consumption. The rainwater-harvesting structures were based on the college's belief that tried-and-tested technologies used by the people for several hundred years to provide safe drinking water should be respected and applied on a large scale. Rainwater is therefore gathered from the flat rooftops and channelled to water storage tanks, usually situated underground. In an arid region such as Tilonia, water and its adequate storage and supply are critical to the very existence of the community. The new system is inexpensive and provides a year-round water supply, even when the monsoon rainfall is low, thus safeguarding emergency needs. One beneficial outcome of the system is that in several rural primary schools the attendance of girls has improved because they do not have to spend hours walking several kilometres to collect drinking water. The system has also led to wasteland reclamation.

There is no doubt that the presence of the Barefoot College and its activities have had a tremendous impact on Tilonia and other outlying rural settlements, influencing every aspect of people's lives. Lifting the surrounding population out of the vicious circle of poverty and helplessness, the college has facilitated a revival of traditional technologies and applied them on a wider scale to solve problems that have baffled scientists, engineers, environmentalists and politicians for years.

Above: A residential block arranged in a traditional courtyard format, with a semicircular stage at its centre.

Barefoot Architects: The campus was
constructed using local stone with
the participation of the community.

Barefoot Architects: Geodesic domes
are covered in a variety of materials
according to their various functions.

Barefoot Architects: The uses of
the domes include pathology labs,
guest houses and classrooms.

Barefoot Architects: As in the dining
hall, simple interiors complement the
cubic forms of the campus buildings.

Barefoot Architects: The crafts
centre encourages traditional skills,
which are used throughout the campus.

Barefoot Architects: [Top] One of over two hundred 'Homes for the Homeless' in the Tilonia area.

[Bottom] Over 350 rainwater-harvesting structures were built with the help of the local community.

Barefoot Architects: [Top] Solar panels are used to pump water from wells to overhead tanks.

[Bottom] The college campus is entirely solar-powered, allowing enormous savings on utilities.

Barefoot Architects: Traditional
decoration in one of the residential
courtyards of the campus.

KAHERE EILA POULTRY FARMING SCHOOL

—

—

—

—

KOLIAGBE, GUINEA

This project has received an Award because it draws on traditional local planning relationships, with a courtyard dominated by a central tree articulating teaching and accommodation spaces. Local materials are combined with sophisticated structural elements, strengthening the resources available to local craftsmen. Distinguished by clarity of form and appropriateness of scale, the solution is a fine example of an elegantly humble yet modern architecture that successfully crosses the boundaries of local Guinean and Nordic traditions and, in the process, avoids mimicry.

It is rare that a piece of architecture can bridge distinct cultures and building methods while maintaining the local characteristics of its context. In those few instances where a harmony is achieved, the results can provide a rewarding range of benefits and outcomes. For a small agricultural school in Guinea, West Africa – the result of an unconventional chain of events and human contacts leading from Africa to Hungary to Finland and back to Africa – a humble yet elegant design has proved an unequivocal success.

Built on a poultry farm in Koliagbe near Kindia, a town 120 kilometres inland from the coast of Guinea, the educational complex was made possible through the support given to local initiatives by Eila Kivekäs, the Finnish patron who funded the project. Its design, by Finnish architects Heikkinen-Komonen, combines the timber structures typical of Finland's native architecture with local materials, improved by simple technological advances.

In the early 1980s Alpha Diallo, a Guinean agronomist, and his uncle, Bachir Diallo, a veterinarian, discussed the idea of creating a poultry farm to address the problem of the Guinean diet's lack of protein, a nutrient that is found in high levels in chickens. Both men earned scholarships to study in Europe, Bachir going to France and then Italy, Alpha to Hungary. There, Alpha developed an interest in the Finnish language, which is related to Hungarian, leading to his translation of the Finnish epic poem, *The Kalevala*, into Fulani, the language of his ethnic group. On a visit to Finland, Alpha met Eila Kivekäs. When Alpha died suddenly in Finland in 1984, Kivekäs arranged for his body to be returned to Guinea to be buried.

Soon afterwards Bachir, by then in Canada, received a phone call from Mrs Kivekäs. She proposed that he return to Guinea – where a change of political regime had created favourable conditions for private initiatives – and create, with her support, the poultry improvement project that Alpha had discussed with her. The poultry farm was started in 1986, and in 1989 Kivekäs founded a development association called Indigo, based in Mali town, which went into partnership with the poultry farm.

One of the primary aims of the poultry farm was education. Local farmers knew little about issues such as increasing production, improving the quality of the meat and preventing infestations, so the school began by instructing groups of between twenty and twenty-five people. Later, agricultural students and professionals started to visit the school. Once trainees, students and researchers began to come regularly, the poultry farm's facilities could no longer accommodate them. In 1997 Kivekäs proposed to Bachir, as director of the poultry farm, that amenities be provided near the main part of the farm.

Kivekäs' involvement with the project partly explains the thinking behind the programme. She was intent on creating an energy-saving, climatically comfortable building that would present a workable alternative to the fired-brick walls and tin roofs of local structures, while encouraging the involvement of local craftsmen and exploring the potential of local materials for good design. She had commissioned Heikkinen-Komonen to work in Guinea on earlier Indigo projects, where the production of local materials had been enhanced by soft technology,

Established in 1997 to help Guineans improve their diet, the school is arranged traditionally with accommodation grouped around a courtyard with a tree at its centre.

Kahere Eila Poultry Farming School

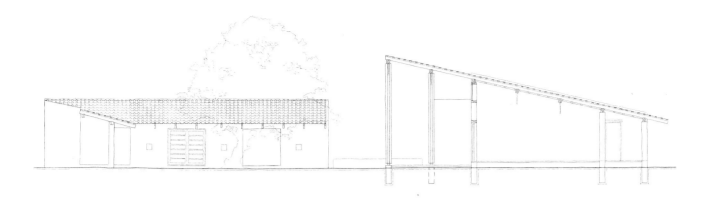

in combination with structural ideas drawn from Finnish traditions and translated to the local craft conditions.

In the areas around Kindia, the oldest form of dwelling, still commonly used, consists of a round construction, made of raw earth-blocks, with a conical, thatched roof. Three distinct types of building – larger structures used as sleeping-cum-common rooms, smaller structures for cooking, and covered areas without walls (known locally as *baré bundi*) for male socializing – are grouped around an open space, usually with a large tree in the centre, where all

the household activities, such as preparation of food and washing of clothes, take place. Close to urban areas, however, most buildings are rectangular, with a hipped tin roof. In recent years, corrugated metal sheeting has rapidly become the preferred roofing material. Concrete blocks are fairly common for construction; but the most common material for walls remains earth-bricks fired in local kilns. Fired bricks are produced by using blocks of earth, excavated nearby, which are shaped with a wooden form. They are dried in the sun, then arranged in piles, which are sealed with mud and burned over

a fire. Those that are not well baked are fired again. The quality of the finished material is poor and the amount of wood required is considerable.

For the new complex, three essential areas were required: a classroom, student quarters for up to twelve people and teachers' quarters. These are organized around a courtyard, at the centre of which is a tree. The plan is based on a 1.2-metre grid, which governs the proportions of the buildings and their relation to each other, imparting a simple but formal elegance to the architecture. The grid is carried through to the window openings, which include fixed windows of 30 by 30 centimetres and openable 160-by-90-centimetre windows, arranged with a rhythm and symmetry that animates the elevations.

The Finnish architects introduced wood-frame technology – posts and rafters joggled and fastened by simple steel elements – in combination with weight-bearing walls made from a double layer of specially developed stabilized earth-blocks. As well as providing energy savings by dispensing with the need for firing, these blocks act as heat collectors, moderating room temperature, and their hard, smooth finish means that they do not need rendering. The wider span of the classroom is covered with the aid of simple metal trusses combined with the wooden beams. The tallest columns, those of the classroom porch, are made of four posts fastened by intermediate wooden blocks and steel bolts, an economical way of overcoming a shortage of long pieces of hardwood.

All primary materials were sourced locally. Wood, including hard acajou and softer samba for the structure and iroko

Top: Cross-section showing the classroom, with its tall entrance portico, facing the students' and teachers' residential blocks across the courtyard.

Centre left and right: The school ensures climatic comfort through low-technology energy-saving methods such as shaded areas and local materials such as stabilized earth-blocks.

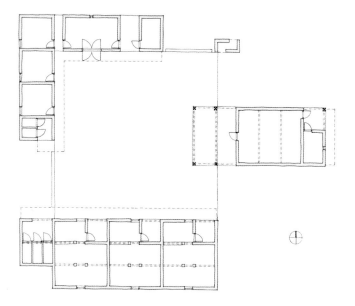

Patron
Eila Kivekäs.

Client
Centre Avicole Kahere-Bachir Diallo,
Director.

Architects
Heikkinen-Komonen Architects-
Mikko Heikkinen and Markku Komonen,
Partners in Charge; Ville Venermo,
Site Manager.

Consultants
Boubakar Barry, Civil Engineer.

Craftsmen
Abdulhaye Djiby Sow, Master Mason;
Suleymane Saouré, Master Carpenter;
Moustapha Souaré, Master Tile Maker.

Commission	1997
Design	1997-98
Construction	1998-99
Occupancy	January 2000
Site Area	3,800m²
Built Area	340m²
Cost	GNF 153,373,000
	(USD 104,000)

for the doors, came from the Guinea forest.
Earth for the blocks and floor tiles was excavated nearby and moulded on site, the blocks
on a hand press, the tiles on wood forms
specially made by the carpenter. Roof tiles
of cement mixed with vegetable sisal were
formed in metal moulds, then submerged
in water tanks made for the purpose. The

surface finishes take into account the
textures offered by the native materials
but areas of bright colour are also introduced: the main elevation of the classroom
is painted deep blue, the entrance porches
of the student quarters bright yellow,
and parts of the teacher's residence
are painted green.

The significance of introducing new
building techniques is best illustrated by
the example of the school's head mason,
who trained in the stabilized earth-block
technique during the construction of the
farm school. He has gone on to use the
blocks in private houses, small industrial
installations and even a mosque, which
has helped boost the area's production
of the blocks.

The rational and simple vocabulary
of the project combines with equally simple
forms of building, resulting in a gentle impact
on the environment. The school and its construction have fostered pride among the
workers and farm staff, and created a positive atmosphere among the students. The
disposition of buildings around a courtyard
is comfortably adapted to the domestic character of the small community studying there,
and gestures like the reversed pitch of the
classroom roof and the large surfaces of
bright colour animate a space that might
otherwise be monotonous.

Top: The plan shows how the Finnish
architects combined traditional
materials with a rational grid based
on a 1.2-metre module.

Centre: In the classroom, metal
trusses are combined with traditional features, such as wooden beams
and the woven mats of the ceiling.

Kahere Eila Poultry Farming School

The water tower with the classroom's
wide portico beyond: the architects
introduced a wood-frame structural
system typical of Finland.

Kahere Eila Poultry Farming School

Natural vegetation around the site
was left intact and the complex's
domestic scale and materials
integrate it with its environment.

Kahere Eila Poultry Farming School

The complex pioneered the use of stabilized blocks made of local earth, which were arranged in double layers to increase their bearing capacity.

096

Kahere Eila Poultry Farming School

While the roofs of the students' and teachers' quarters slope towards the central courtyard, that of the classroom slopes contrapuntally away.

Kahere Eila Poultry Farming School

Simple steel fastenings allow tall
columns to be created from the local
hardwood, offering a way to enhance
local technologies.

Kahere Eila Poultry Farming School

NUBIAN MUSEUM

—

—

—

—

—

—

ASWAN, EGYPT

This project has been cited for an Award for its success in integrating the past, present and future by creating in a single building an educational institution dedicated to Nubian history, a contemporary focus for the revival of Nubian culture and a museum designed to promote and preserve cultural artefacts for the future. The museum was chosen for the high quality of its construction materials, its attention to detail, its successful adaptation of local architectural styles and its stylistic integration into the city of Aswan.

Egypt consists of five well-defined regions: the Delta, the Valley, the Eastern Desert, the Western Desert and Nubia. Taking its name from the ancient Egyptian *nbu*, meaning gold, in reference to the area's famous gold mines, Nubia was historically Egypt's gateway to the rest of Africa and as such an important trading centre. Its people were settlers who subsisted on agriculture, trade and pastoral activities. From the time of the Old Kingdom, circa 2500 BC, Nubia went through alternating periods of independence and domination by Egypt, but by the Twenty-Fifth Dynasty, Nubian rulers enjoyed long periods of self-rule, political stability and economic prosperity. Even the Roman emperors, who showed great interest in Nubia, allowed it to retain independence under their sovereignty. Mainly Christian from the sixth century AD, in the eighth and ninth centuries Nubia gradually began to convert to Islam through intermarriage with Arab traders. Not until the sixteenth century, however, was the conversion complete.

Today, there is no political entity called Nubia. Its lands now lie partly in Egypt and partly in the Sudan. When the Aswan High Dam was opened in 1971, a section of the Nile Valley was flooded to form Lake Nasser,

and most of Nubia's northern region was submerged. In anticipation of this event, 40,000 Nubians were resettled, and a programme of excavation and movement of temples was initiated. In 1960, when the construction of the High Dam commenced, UNESCO launched the International Campaign to Save the Monuments of Nubia, which ran forty archaeological missions from five continents, rescuing twenty-two monuments in twenty years. With the Egyptian government, UNESCO decided to establish the Nubian Museum at Aswan and the Egyptian Civilization Museum in Cairo to exhibit the finds of the excavations.

Displaying three thousand objects found in the UNESCO expeditions and celebrating the culture and civilization of the Nubian region from prehistoric times to the present, the Nubian Museum was opened to the public in December 1997. The project was funded entirely by the Egyptian government. Located in the city of Aswan, on the eastern bank of the Nile, 900 kilometres south of Cairo, the museum is an important centre for museology and the preservation and conservation of archaeological remains from Africa and the Middle East. It also aims to serve as a 'community museum', with an educational

View of the city of Aswan and, in the foreground, the Nubian Museum, designed to preserve the artefacts and culture of the Nubian people displaced by the Aswan High Dam.

section – the first in Egypt – that organizes trips, lectures and workshops for children, and cultural events for the public at large.

Sited near an ancient granite quarry, the museum comprises two essential parts: a three-storey building, and a landscaped outdoor exhibition area that includes examples of Nubian architecture. Traditional Nubian architecture encompasses the great temples, which were simple buildings of granite or stone, and the vernacular structures of the villages, built in mud, mud-brick or stone. Nubian villages are spread along the Nile in clustered terraces, with the principal entrances to houses facing the river. These open onto a courtyard – with raised seating areas called *mastabas* – where rooms are arranged along the far wall, the most important being the *mandara*, or guest room, which has a separate entrance and a catenary roof-vault. Some living rooms – called *khayma*, or tents – are simply open with a flat roof of palm branches.

The museum was essentially built to the design of Dr El-Hakim but executed by the Arab Bureau of Design. It is placed on a ridge to preserve the site's granite rock formations and to provide an open view of two of Aswan's key attractions: the Fatimid Cemetery and the Unfinished Obelisk to the east. The museum's massing follows the terrain's contours, blending well with the surrounding topography, and the hand-textured local sandstone of its exterior façades enhances the building's relationship to the site. The open triangle motif used on the west façade is taken from traditional Nubian architecture and is one of a number of elements subtly incorporated into the design to reflect the local vernacular.

The overall design concept is to lead the visitor through the museum and out to the external spaces, where the history of the Nubian civilization is presented chronologically. Oriented towards the Nile in the same way as traditional Nubian houses, the entrance to the 10,000-square-metre main building is on the west side, where a portico shades the main door from the sun. Entering at ground level, visitors are led down to the main exhibition area in the basement, where they find the museum's centrepiece – a statue of Rameses II (1304–1237 BC), builder of the great temple at Abu Simbel. Also in the basement is a diorama showing the history of the Nubian people. On either side of the exhibition hall are the educational facilities, and five

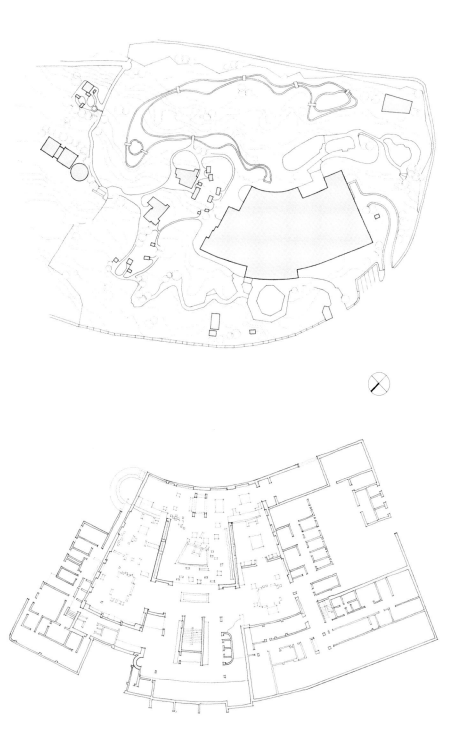

Top: Site plan showing the building and surrounding outdoor areas.
Bottom: Floor plan of the main exhibition area of the museum itself.

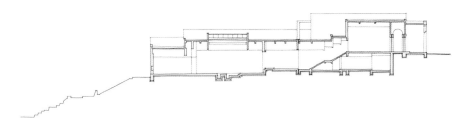

laboratories – papyrus and fabric, organic, metal, inorganic and a fumigation lab – as well as the main storage areas and exhibition workshops. On the ground floor are the main entrance hall, shops, a temporary exhibition hall and a 150-seat lecture theatre. The first floor holds a cafeteria, library, administration offices and a meeting room. Like the façades, the walls and floors of the interior spaces are clad in a local material – in this case pink granite – while the ceilings of the exhibition areas are open-timber grids, arranged to reflect the layout of the museum and providing maximum flexibility for installation of lights and services. The spaces of the museum are generous and the flow around the exhibits is clear and easy.

The outdoor exhibition area is intended to represent the Nile Valley. It includes a cave housing prehistoric drawings of animals, a traditional Nubian house, an outdoor theatre for five hundred people, two shrines – the *maqqam* of Saida Zeinab and the *maqqam* of the 77 *walis* (governors) – a *musalla* (place of prayer), and several graves, said to be Roman, Fatimid and Coptic in origin. A water canal represents the River Nile, which is surrounded by local flora and fauna.

The museum is successful in its relationship to Aswan and popular among the city's residents, who are proud of their museum and feel that it reflects their way of life. In this sense, it plays an important role in informing both Egyptian and international visitors about the importance and uniqueness of Nubian culture. As a centre of learning for all people, young and old, local and foreign, the museum preserves an ancient civilization for the future and forms a focal point of community life.

Clients
Nubian Antiquities Salvage Fund: The Supreme Council of Antiquities – Gaballah Ali Gaballah, Secretary General: Nubian Museum – Ossama A W Abdel Meguid, Director.

Sponsor
UNESCO; ICOM – International Council of Museums.

Architect
Mahmoud El-Hakim.

Consultants
The Arab Bureau for Design and Technical Consultation – Mohamad Yusri Abdel Khalik, Project Architect; Architectural Team – Ahmed Kamal Abdel Fattah, Mohamed Tharwat, Lilly George.

Museum Display Designer
Pedro Ramírez Vásquez.

Landscape
Dr Werkmeister & M Heimer Landscape Architects – Hans Friedrich Werkmeister, Principal: Sites International Landscape Architects – Laila El-Masry Stino, Principal, with Maher Stino and Khaled Mostafa.

Contractors
El-Nasr General Contracting Company – Hassan Allam, Construction: Silver Knight Exhibitions Ltd, interiors.

Commission   1979
Design Phase I   1983–85
Design Phase II   September 1984–
                  October 1995
Construction   1986–97
Occupancy   November 1997
Site Area   50,000m²
Built Area   10,110m²
Cost   EGP 57,000,000
                  (USD 15,000,000)

Top: A cross-section through the building shows how it steps down its steep site to create a clearly legible flow through the exhibits.

Bottom: Schoolchildren learn about Nubian culture from a topographical model – part of an extensive education programme at the heart of the museum's activities.

105

Nubian Museum: The complex at night
[top] and at dawn [bottom]. Sandstone
cladding blends into the landscape.

106

Nubian Museum: The entrance faces
the Nile, as in traditional Nubian
structures.

107

Nubian Museum: From the entrance
visitors are led down a flight of
stairs to the main exhibition area.

مدينة الخنيدى
THE SETTLEMENT OF IKHMINDI

Nubian Museum: An interior exhibition area
[top] and the popular diorama of Nubian
daily life [bottom].

109

Nubian Museum: From the interior,
a sequence of exterior spaces leads
to the outdoor exhibition area.

110

Nubian Museum: The outdoor area
represents the Nile Valley, with a
canal symbolizing the River Nile.

Nubian Museum: Alongside local
building types (top), indigenous
plants are featured (bottom).

SOS CHILDREN'S VILLAGE

—

—

—

—

—

AQABA, JORDAN

The project has received an Award for creating a pleasant and attractive environment scaled to the needs of children. The village's well-defined layout creates generous communal outdoor areas, shaded courtyards and gardens that serve as safe playgrounds for the children and form a desirable oasis within the arid, desert surroundings. In its sober and modern interpretation of local vernacular traditions, this thoughtful and integrated architecture has set a precedent in both cultural and aesthetic terms.

On the outskirts of Aqaba, Jordan's outlet to the Red Sea, a sensitive building has fused a modern design vocabulary with a renewal of the local building vernacular to create a haven for orphaned children. Sincere, thoughtfully scaled and arranged and environmentally friendly, the village succeeds in providing a comfortable place where children can feel at home.

Historical texts record settlement around Aqaba in the late ninth century, but the modern seaport retains little of its past. The only traditional buildings remaining are a Mamluk fort, built in the early sixteenth century, and the house of Al Sharif Hussain of Makkah, built in the early twentieth century. As a result, Aqaba has little distinct architectural or urban character. The prevalent forms are dictated by the use of concrete and, because the industrialized building materials favoured by Jordan's construction industry have marginalized the input of local communities, Aqaba has few local architects and no professional, trained labour force.

The SOS Villages International programme is based on the concept of providing an environment in which orphaned children can enjoy living conditions that are as close as possible to those of normal family life. A prerequisite of the programme is that villages should be integrated into an existing urban community, so that children are not isolated from their context. The Aqaba SOS complex is the second such scheme to be built in Jordan, and was designed by Jafar Tukan and completed in 1991. Houses were created to accommodate nine children each – seventy-two in all – minded by a dedicated woman who becomes a surrogate 'mother' figure. The children are provided with private meals and tutoring, and have a sibling-like relationship with other children in the unit. Father figures include the 'village father' (the director of the village, who lives on the premises with his real family), his assistant or deputy, and other men working in the village, such as the gardener and maintenance man. One objective of the project was to integrate the village with the surrounding community by establishing public and social interaction points – a pharmacy and supermarket, which generate a small income for the village, and a sports centre and kindergarten.

The complex comprises eight family houses, a staff house, an administration

The SOS Children's Village in Aqaba is the second such complex in Jordan, implementing a programme of providing care for orphans in an environment similar to normal family homes.

SOS Children's Village

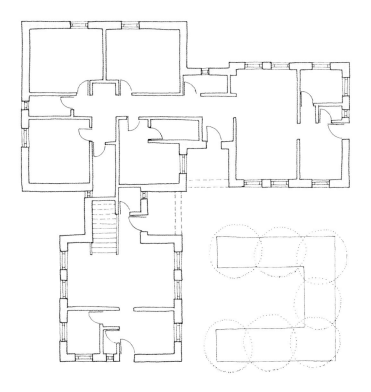

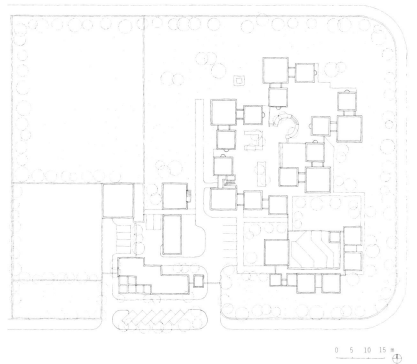

building, a guest house and the village director's residence. All are planned around a 'village square' and connected via pedestrian paths, gardens and alleyways. Vaulted archways lead to shaded courts, while gardens surround the buildings on all sides. The shared facilities are located on the southern border of the site, close to the main road. Because summer temperatures can reach uncomfortable heights, the complex is arranged in clusters of buildings, surrounded by breezy outdoor spaces for living and playing, animated by lush vegetation and shading trees.

Details that enliven the exterior spaces include solid-wood window frames and *mashrabiyyas*, or screens, which filter the light of the harsh sun. Doors are painted in bright colours. Stone façades and arches and the open courts and spaces provide both an intimate and private feel and the possibility of outdoor living. Within, the houses offer open, flexible spaces that generously accommodate the children. Jordan's warm climate means that no heating is required and domestic hot water is provided by solar panels. Traditional ventilation techniques have been implemented and the dwellings

Top and bottom left: Floor plan of a typical 'family house' and site plan of the village, comprising eight houses, each for nine children, arranged around a central square.

Top and centre right: The buildings feature traditional cooling techniques, such as wind funnels, wooden screens and shading trellises.

enjoy good thermal insulation. As a result, maintenance requirements are minimal.

Perhaps the most innovative aspect of the design, however, is its use of a traditional cladding of random granite stones. Drawing on the few remaining examples of traditional buildings in Aqaba's old town, the architect's exploration of stonework has allowed a reinterpretation of traditional architectural characteristics, using local materials and labour-intensive, traditional technology. A study was implemented to look at the best way of building with the natural stone from the mountains around Aqaba. Piles of stones were collected by hand, since 'machines could spoil the texture and look of the natural stones'. The process was simple, but time-consuming: each morning four teams went to collect the stones; at the end of the day the contractor's engineer approved the shape and size of the stones prior to transporting them to the site. The contractor was then faced with the task of building the facings according the architect's design. The architect specified that the stone was 'not to be mechanically cut or dressed but [had to] remain completely natural'. Several days were spent on site with a local builder to construct numerous samples until a final version was approved. Having mastered the process, the builder and contractor were able to train others, contributing to a revival of traditional building techniques. At the same time, modern elements were introduced, with wooden structural elements replaced by pre-cast concrete.

The architecture's modest synthesis of vernacular and modern forms is exemplary in showing how designers should give full consideration to regional architecture in order to understand the environmental or ecological decisions that have been made in the past, and to learn how they might be applied to the present and future. According to Mohammed Balqar of Aqaba's special economic zone authority, the use of stone in the village has created a precedent for local building: 'Before the SOS Children's Village …people did not know the importance of good architecture.' He now takes people to the complex to show how 'our urban areas should look'. The village's architecture is being used as a guideline for developing traditional architecture and has given local authorities an added incentive to upgrade the old town's infrastructure, which they now view as the heart of Aqaba's urban fabric. Private properties must now be built in an architectural style that is defined as a mixture of modern and local, using materials from around Aqaba.

Architecture is at its highest form of accomplishment when it can shelter humans in a way that is sensitive to their culture, their community and their surroundings. In this case, the design fosters the integration of the children within the village and the outside community. The complex provides the children with an exceptional environment, and the village feels as if it is owned and run by them. This gives them security and happiness, which is in turn reflected in the large measure of civility, discipline and good manners that can be witnessed there. On a broader scale, the village has had a great impact on the local urban environment, and proposes a more sensitive approach to design and planning through a careful process of research.

Client
SOS Children's Village Association of Jordan.

Architects
Jafar Tukan & Partners — Jafar Tukan, Principal Designer; Ralph Montgomery, Architectural Design; Munib Kayyali, Structural Engineer; Adel Taher, Mechanical Engineer; Azmi Sherif, Electrical Engineer.

Contractor
Ammoun Maintenance Contracting Co.

Design	March 1988– January 1989
Construction	Feb 1989–Jun 1991
Occupation	August 1991
Site area	20,000m²
Built area	2,700m²
Cost	JOD 1,211,750 (USD 1,730,000)

Bottom left and right: The village includes both generous spaces for enclosed outdoor living and spacious and flexible interiors.

117

SOS Children's Village: [Top] The
village has a supermarket and pharmacy, which generate a support income.

[Bottom] Despite its urban setting,
the complex provides secluded
private spaces.

SOS Children's Village: The network
of pathways and gardens gives
children freedom to roam and play

119

SOS Children's Village: A facing of
granite from the nearby mountains
attunes the complex to its setting.

120

121

SOS Children's Village: Stone for the
cladding was collected by hand and
hand cut to maintain its texture.

122

123

SOS Children's Village: The complex
has inspired a revival of traditional
building techniques in Aqaba.

124

SOS Children's Village: Interiors are
simple but comfortable, enlivened by
the activities of the children.

OLBİA SOCIAL CENTRE

—

—

—

—

—

ANTALYA, TURKEY

The project has been given an Award for its intimate human scale, its function as a bridge between several architectural styles and geographic areas of an existing university campus, and its innovative fusion of contemporary architectural elements with local materials. The complex has created an attractive place where students and teachers can meet and exchange ideas. Using symbolic, historical and cultural elements, the centre creates new connections to the past, showing how today's architects can look deep into their own cultures.

In 1997 the architect Cengiz Bektaş was invited to give a presentation and a lecture at the Akdeniz Üniversitesi in Antalya about the town's old city. The lecture helped to raise awareness among the university's staff that their campus lacked identity in its buildings and spaces, and that this resulted in poor communication between teachers and students. A year later the university commissioned the architect to design a new social centre to act as a binding element for the disparate parts of the campus.

Lying on the western fringes of Antalya, the main city on Turkey's central Mediterranean coast, the university has a modern campus, with different faculties scattered around a large plot, connected by wide roads and boulevards. Its buildings, standing between six and thirteen storeys high, are in a variety of modern styles, bearing little relation to their context and providing no sense of individual character. The campus stands in marked contrast to the old city, founded by Attalus II of Pergamon in the first century BC, which bears many physical reminders of its various historical rulers, including a Roman harbour and fortress, the Yivli minaret and gracious old Ottoman

hayat houses. This dense urban fabric is based around cobble-stone streets, which curve to adapt to the extreme slopes of the city, with houses irregularly shaped to follow the streets. Construction techniques have changed little over the centuries, and most buildings are made of local stone, giving a sense of unity to structures from various historical periods. Empty water channels along some streets are part of an old system that irrigated private gardens with water from the northern mountains.

The concept of the new centre was based on the architect's belief that, in order for a sense of community to flourish, it is imperative that people from different disciplines should meet and exchange ideas in a relaxed atmosphere – much in the way that past civilizations used a common space, such as the Greek agora, the Roman forum or the Oriental bazaar. He also stressed the importance of 'incidental' and informal learning, noting that students learn more from each other than from the classroom. Accordingly, the main objective was to create adequate places for students to interact both with each other and with teaching staff in a comfortable and informal way.

View of the Olbia Social Centre, commissioned to create a social hub to tie together the discordant buildings of the university campus seen in the background.

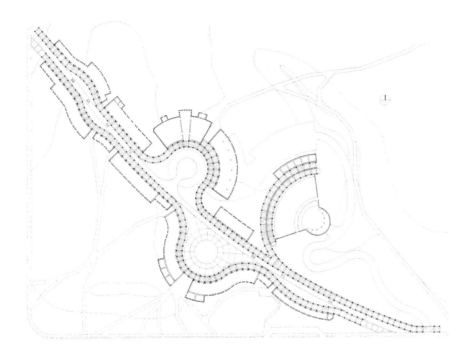

The complex is designed according to the layout of a traditional bazaar, with a series of buildings arranged around a central axis formed by a pathway. This is divided centrally by a water channel, which flows over gentle waterfalls from the highest point of the site, humidifying and cooling the surrounding spaces. In two places, the pathway widens to create outdoor focal points for the various functions. The space to the north contains a large pool of still water, surrounded by an auditorium complex and restaurant. To the south, a small pit of stepped seats, with a water fountain at its centre, can be used for individual reflection or for interaction within small groups, overlooked by a clock tower. Around this space are arranged cafés, and book, stationery and various other shops. At other stages along the central walkway are rooms for student clubs, an exhibition area and a sports club. Covering both sides of the path, curving, linear pergolas balance and integrate indoor and outdoor space. To the east, an open-air amphitheatre with seating for 1,200 people is used for performances and a wide range of social and cultural activities, not just by the students but also by the residents of Antalya, helping to integrate the university campus into the surrounding community. A series of paths connects the main axis with the bus station, the student hostel, the rector's office and neighbouring university buildings, making the complex the hub and visual focus of the campus.

The flow of spaces and masses along the gently curving pathway, with water elements as a regulating concept, gives an ever-changing aspect from both inside and outside the complex, enhancing the functional and experiential qualities of pedestrian circulation in the campus. The fragmentation of the accommodation into independent components of varying proportions serves to humanize the scale and means that each building is adapted to the spatial requirements of its function. All of the buildings are designed on a basic repetitive module of 3.6 metres, allowing for flexibility in the future division of the spaces according to changing needs and functions, and forming an organizational element for the various architectural spaces.

The project responds to the surrounding environment, adapting the simple traditional techniques and materials of the old city. Allowing workers and craftsmen to put their own knowledge and methods to use during construction, the architect also taught them some of the old techniques, reviving building traditions in the area. The predominantly one-storey buildings were constructed mainly from granite stone, quarried from the site during excavation of the foundations and then rough-cut *in situ* and combined with reinforced-concrete beams to form load-bearing walls. Resting on the load-bearing walls, the convex timber ceiling structure borrows its materials and technique from Antalya's ancient shipbuilding industry, fostering pride in the region's history and achievements. Resting on this structure, the roofs slope towards the water channel at the centre of the pathways, and are clad with traditional red ceramic tiles. The wooden ceiling beams of the latticed pergolas are supported on one side by the walls of the buildings and on the other by prefabricated concrete columns, which carry light and sound fixtures. The columns also bear copper plaques that give information about important Turkish cultural figures, enabling

Top left: Plan of the complex. The facilities line a central spine divided by a water channel to form two walkways.

Top and centre right: At two points the walkways diverge to enclose circular outdoor areas which act as focal points for student clubs and cafés.

Client
Akdeniz Üniversitesi.

Architect
Cengiz Bektaş.

Consultant
Eral Soner, Civil Engineer.

Contractor
Baki Yapı Malzemeleri İnşaat Sanayii
ve Ticaret Ltd Sti — Attila Türkoğlu,
Site Engineer.

Commission   1998
Design   1998
Construction   1998
Occupation   September 1999
Site area   12,000m²
Built area   3,641m²
Cost   USD 728,000

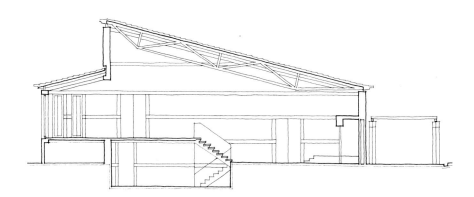

students to learn about different aspects of contemporary Turkey in an informal manner. Unity in building materials, construction techniques and details helps to bring harmony to the various volumes and functions. What counts, as in traditional arrangements, is the whole experience, the movement through spaces, and perceptions from different angles.

A number of trees existed on the site prior to building, and the design for the most part has worked around and preserved them. When construction commenced, the architect added more indigenous trees, shrubs and flowers, which create an ever-changing environment due to the plants' growth cycle and the different seasons. Areas of grass have also been introduced, as well as climbing plants around the pergolas, which, when mature, will provide shading for the hot summer months.

The name 'Olbia' – an old word for city – was chosen by public vote, encapsulating the project's traditional and social qualities. The centre is almost always full of

students and teachers, who show an unmistakable sense of enjoyment and relaxation and appreciate the intimate quality of the complex. Teaching staff and administration alike are proud to have the centre, which is unique among Turkish universities, and rectors of other universities who have visited the Olbia Social Centre have been inspired to plan similar projects on their own campuses.

The project has achieved – and surpassed – the university's objectives by connecting the scattered buildings of the campus, bringing together teachers and students from different disciplines in a relaxed environment, and metaphorically linking contemporary life with Turkey's historical past. In so doing, it forms a catalyst for activities that promote the social, educational and intellectual development of students. The project provides a role model for an architecture that revives traditional design principles, building techniques and symbols, while learning and adopting appropriate ideas from modern life.

Top and centre: Cross-section through the southern outdoor area and a typical building: all accommodation is based on a module that unifies the various spaces.

Olbia Social Centre

129

Olbia Social Centre: The complex was
designed on a more human scale than
the campus's multi-storey blocks.

Olbia Social Centre: The amphitheatre
combines modernity and tradition —
concrete seating and stone walls.

131

Olbia Social Centre: Timber trusses
refer to Antalya's shipbuilding
history.

132

Olbia Social Centre: Pergolas shade
the gently curving walkways, which
are bordered by local plants.

133

Olbia Social Centre: Water unifies
the complex, flowing through pools
and fountains and along the channel.

Olbia Social Centre: Informal meeting
places create a relaxed setting for
student-teacher interaction.

135

Olbia Social Centre: The amphitheatre
is used by the wider community as
well as for student performances.

Olbia Social Centre: The varying
spaces flow into each other, forming
a series of shifting perspectives.

BAGH-E-
FERDOWSI

—

—

—

—

—

TEHRAN, IRAN

The project has been chosen for its innovative approach to environmental design, which limits urban development and promotes an awareness of conservation and nature amongst the urban population of Tehran. As a setting for outdoor recreational and cultural pursuits, the park provides spaces for contemplation, family recreation and social interaction, and for the appreciation of local culture and entertainment. Imaginative use of materials, playful sculptures and indigenous landscaping draw on the best traditions of garden design in the region to create a refreshing change to the spread of stifling and homogeneous urban forms.

Since the 1950s, rapid population growth in Tehran has created huge pressure for land on which to build and resulted in the destruction of many of the public and private gardens that once graced the city. As part of a wider range of measures to promote urban improvement and limit the sprawl of the city, Tehran Municipality has supported efforts to protect the natural environment of the Alborz Mountains that form the northern perimeter of Tehran. During the late 1970s, a 12-hectare park – the Jamshidieh Stone Garden – created at the foot of the Alborz Mountains, proved to be highly popular. As a result, in 1992, the municipality commissioned the park's architects – Baft-e-Shahr Consulting Engineers – to prepare a wider study for the outlying areas north of Tehran. The aim of the project was to create a green interface between city and nature and to engender an understanding of the importance of the environment, in both physical and cultural terms, among urban residents. The first part of the study to be implemented was a 30-hectare park – Bagh-e-Ferdowsi – adjacent to the Jamshidieh Stone Garden.

Set at an altitude of between 1,800 and 2,100 metres above sea level, the site of Bagh-e-Ferdowsi is in Tang Hesarak Valley, comprising a series of steep south-facing gullies, scattered with loose rocks and boul-

ders. In order to assess the full potential of the site, the design team camped there for a month, recording the key natural features through photographs and drawings. Ideas for the enhancement of the landscape through the introduction of paths, steps, terraces, squares, sculptures and planting were developed in a series of sketches on transparent overlays on the photographs. Once finalized, these drawn overlays formed the basis for marking out in lime the proposed interventions to the site, to ensure compatibility with the existing natural features. These design exercises were carried out in consultation with a range of different interest groups, including the Ministry of Education, the Organization for Natural Resources and mountaineers.

The design emerged, to a large extent, from the natural topography and features of the rocky slopes, so that the final scheme is very much in harmony with its surroundings. Apart from intensive planting, the primary intervention is a series of stone-paved paths and steps rising up the slope of the hill, with views out over the city. Along these paths, areas for sitting, refreshment and entertainment have been created within the natural topography, including four cultural houses, built to represent the distinctive architectural and decorative styles of the Azeri,

Bagh-e-Ferdowsi was initiated by the municipality of Tehran to form a green buffer zone between the city and the untouched landscape of the Alborz Mountains to the north.

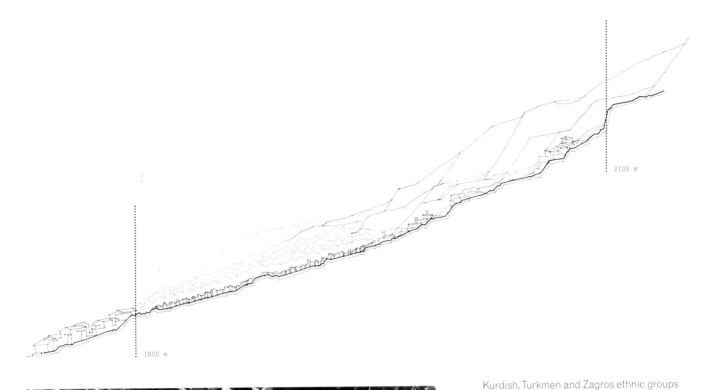

2100 m

1800 m

Kurdish, Turkmen and Zagros ethnic groups in Iran. The paths link up with others leading to a sculpture garden being developed to the east, or to hiking trails into the upper valleys – the steep, 40-degree incline of the site provides vigorous training for mountain climbers and exercise enthusiasts.

The landscaping of the routes is designed to explore a number of themes, both cultural and natural. The entry point for the park is a paved open space dominated by an imposing statue of Ferdowsi (940–c 1020), the great Iranian epic poet after whom the park is named. From this space, a wide stepped pathway forms a 'cascade passage', which branches into a network of pathways across the site, bordered by a variety of indigenous plants chosen for their form, colour and suitability to the environment. All existing native trees and shrubs on the site were saved where possible. Shade trees are complemented by a rich mix of shrubs to create a varied environment. Between the paved paths, copses of trees have been planted to provide both shade and swathes of colour during the changing seasons.

Every effort was made to minimize excavation or back-filling for the various buildings, paths and terraces. The primary material is rough-hewn stone, collected from the site or quarried from higher up

Top: A cross-section shows the progression from the urban context, at 1,800 metres, to the more mountainous terrain at 2,100 metres.

Bottom: Having camped on site for a month, the design team was inspired by the topography to create a park that enhances rather than transforms its natural setting.

139

Bagh-e-Ferdowsi

the mountain ridge. Retaining walls and terraces have been constructed in undulating patterns, according to the size and shape of the stones, thereby minimizing cutting. Many large boulders have been used as focal points for the various incidental spaces along the routes. In a number of places dramatic natural rocky outcrops have been imaginatively sculpted into recognizable forms such as fish, lizards and bears, creating an environment where respect for nature can be playfully developed among the young. Likewise, the location and form of the various cultural houses respond to the existing topography, and the contours of the site have been exploited to create significant open spaces, such as two amphitheatres.

Special attention has been paid to the design and furnishing of the cultural houses, conceived as places to explore different aspects of ethnic identity, including crafts, music, poetry and history. Traditional materials have been used to reflect the distinct way of life of the groups represented: for example, red stone was brought in from Azerbaijan for use in and around the Azeri house; the Zagros house takes the form of an open-sided nomadic tent; while the Turkmen cultural house comprises a series of circular spaces with distinctive domed roofs, derived from traditional yurts. Used as a restaurant, the Turkmen house has a large central fireplace, around which live music performances take place. An adjoining stone-paved terrace is used for picnics or outdoor barbecues.

The use of water – one of the main organizing elements in traditional gardens, which were created as oases – reflects its symbolic significance in Persian culture. With no natural source of water on the site, the designers ingeniously created water channels leading from drinking fountains in the public spaces. These sinuous channels bisect the paths and serve to drain rainwater

from paths and terraces. Lighting also represents an important aspect of the design, with all of the principal paths to the summit lit by pole-mounted lights. The distinctive patterns made by the lights against the slopes of the Alborz Mountains are now something of a landmark from the city below.

The completed project was inaugurated in 1997. It enjoys huge popularity among the public: many thousands of visitors arrive at weekends and, on a typical spring evening, young people, couples and families meander along the paths, chat in the meeting places, or picnic on the slopes. Many enjoy the park's sense of peace and tranquillity. For others, it provides a space for social interaction, recreation and entertainment, either in the amphitheatres or in the four cultural houses. Young people, who may wish to climb to the upper slopes of the park, have an opportunity for exercise in an unspoiled environment, free from the pollution of Tehran. For them, the project provides an important social focus and a sense of freedom. The park has also set a precedent for environmental design in Iran: a number of municipalities have sent their staff to study the park as a basis for their own initiatives, and it has been used as a model of environmental design on professional courses.

The development of Bagh-e-Ferdowsi has had a direct and positive impact on the surrounding urban environment. Not only has it alleviated pressure for development on the untouched slopes of the Alborz Mountains, but it has also created a unique environment where nature, people and culture are able to meet and thrive. As such, Bagh-e-Ferdowsi represents a creative reinterpretation of the traditional Persian 'paradise' garden adapted to modern needs, and pays testimony to the importance of environmental design within the overall process of urban development.

Clients
Tehran Municipality – Gholamhossein Karbaschi, former Mayor; Abolghassem Ashouri, former Deputy Mayor for Technical Affairs and Development.

Architects
Baft-e-Shahr Consulting Architects and Urban Planners – Gholamreza Pasban Hazrat, Principal; Fathali Farhad Abozzia, Landscape Design; Ahmad Ghahraman, Botanist; Fariba Gharaï, Mojgan Bahmanyar and Mohammad Naseripour, Design of Cultural Houses; Ahmad Hadad Kaveh, Mechanical Engineer; Aliasghar Ghahramani, Electrical Engineer; Hossein Hamed Azimi, Quantity Surveyor; Hamid Ghaffari, Site Survey; Harmik Khodagholi Araghi and Farhad Mohammed Sohi, Site Supervisors.

Sculptors
Nasser Houshmand-Vaziri (thirty sculptures) and Simin Ekrami (two sculptures).

Consultant
Organization for Technical and Engineering Consultancy of the City of Tehran.

Contractor
Helochin Company

Design   1992
Construction   1993–96
Completion   1997
Cost   USD 2,700,000

Top: Extensive use was made of the rock that scattered the slopes of the site, which was the primary material of the paths and walls.

Top right: The park offers views over Tehran and, in turn, forms a landmark from the city, especially when illuminated at night.

141

Bagh-e-Ferdowsi: A family picnics on
the slopes — the park is an important
social and recreational focus.

142

Bagh-e-Ferdowsi: The design's key
feature is the network of paths that
lead up the slope.

144

Bagh-e-Ferdowsi: The paths are punctuated with areas for sitting, refreshment or performances.

146

Bagh-e-Ferdowsi: Resting places along
the routes are often created around
large, sometimes sculpted, boulders.

Bagh-e-Ferdowsi: Four pavilions
explore Iran's Azeri, Kurdish,
Turkmen and Zagros cultures.

DATAI HOTEL

PULAU LANGKAWI, MALAYSIA

The Aga Khan Award for Architecture

This project has received an Award for its ecological approach to coastal development. Sensitive siting of its buildings away from the beachfront, and careful adaptation to the prevailing topography, vegetation and climate have allowed nature to reclaim the terrain after construction. The project attains a level of quality — both in terms of materials and experiences — rarely achieved in tourist developments. It is a successful combination of talent, stylistic refinement, attention to detail, the use of traditional forms and materials, and the rigour of modern architecture.

All too frequently the opportunity to marry luxury tourism to ecological sensitivity is disregarded by private investors in favour of easier, more cost-effective or more sensational developments. Occasionally, however, a project is ambitious enough in conception and outlook to accommodate the needs of the most demanding clients and the most fragile environments. The Datai, a five-star hotel on a popular tourist resort island in northern Malaysia, is an example of just how far developer and architect can go to achieve a healthy symbiosis between rich terrain and built form, tradition and tourism, and vernacular styles and Modernism.

The Australian architect, Kerry Hill, was involved in the site selection from the outset. Comprising 750 hectares of untouched tropical rainforest, the site has several important natural features: the sea and coral reef, the beach, the rainforest itself, and a well-developed and sensitive ecosystem of swamps, streams and wildlife. A further distinctive element in the terrain is a ridge, which drops sharply to the waterfront. The architect was committed to safeguarding these natural features. Early in the design process, he sited the hotel away from the beach to minimize its impact on the waterfront, placing the complex instead on the ridge to provide spectacular views and leave more of the forest undisturbed. The hotel is thus in the heart of the forest yet with easy access to the waterfront. Another significant design decision was to fragment the hotel into free-standing buildings, with pavilions and isolated villas, which helped to reduce the mass of the complex and its impact on

the site, and allowed flexibility in siting the buildings to minimize the felling of trees.

The hotel contains eighty-four rooms, and forty villas. The rooms are broken up into four blocks of accommodation, arranged around a swimming pool and linked by open walkways. The free-standing villas are located on the lower slopes of the site, between the ridge and the beach. The public areas of the complex – such as restaurants, a spa and a beach house – are distributed around the site in pavilions, a form drawn from the local building vernacular, which features a flexible demarcation of interior and exterior spaces, allowing air circulation and adaptability to suit the time of day or season. The various elements of the complex also follow local building traditions in being built either on stilts or heavy stone bases to protect them from ground damp, and in the use of generous overhangs to keep off rain. The resort makes extensive use of local building materials, notably timber, due to the great natural resources of the forest, where an array of good building woods is readily available.

The task of building in a tropical forest is a difficult responsibility. When trees are cleared to make way for a building, there is a 'festering wound' effect whereby species on the perimeter that are not resistant to ultraviolet rays begin to burn out. This can be mitigated through the planting of 'pioneering' species – trees that grow very fast, blocking the ultraviolet rays to the adjoining trees and allowing existing (often slow-growing) species to survive. The architect designed and modulated the buildings in the resort in consideration of this process,

Top left: The Datai aims to provide all the facilities of a luxury hotel without harming its rainforest site: the hotel is almost invisible in its setting.

Top right: To minimize the complex's impact on the waterfront, the hotel was pulled back onto a ridge in the heart of the forest.

150

Datai Hotel

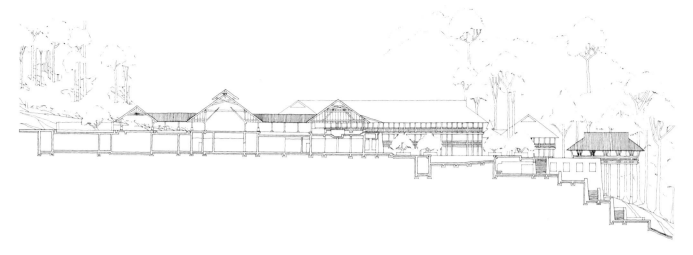

carefully positioning them to reduce tree felling. Trained elephants rather than bulldozers were used to fell the trees because they can penetrate the forest with minimal damage, and trees felled from the site were recycled for use within the structures.

Other measures taken to ensure the minimum of disruption to the surroundings include a recycling plant, localized soak pits and septic tanks that allow filtered seepage of water back into the forest. The resort has its own bore wells to supply water, and some rain is harvested. Water has been intelli-

gently channelled through the site and is collected in natural creeks and runaways. These features were safeguarded and, when building over a creek was unavoidable, the structure was designed as a bridge to allow the creek to pass below it. The natural topography and storm-water drainage system of the site has been left undisturbed, allowing the original catchment and flow patterns to be maintained.

The technology used for construction is an elegant synthesis of traditional building methods and contemporary approaches. For

example, the unplaned tree trunks used for columns, trusses and beams, are assembled with more care than they would be in a traditional building. Alignments, finishing, joinery, the materials used and the way they are combined all coalesce to create a sophisticated structural vocabulary. The level of finish achieved is unusual in Malaysia and has set a precedent for the region's construction quality.

Maintenance and ageing are important considerations in a finely wrought building, but the complex was designed to weather

Top: The architect also fragmented the hotel into a number of free-standing pavilions, villas and accommodation blocks to reduce the mass of the buildings.

Bottom: The structure is integrated with its setting through extensive use of local wood and other traditional materials, all carefully and elegantly detailed.

naturally. A pleasing patina of age is already evident on exposed wooden members and railings, which are not painted or polished but allowed to age gracefully – a natural characteristic of the local hardwoods. Similarly, the stone used for the base of the buildings allows creepers to grow naturally over it and is hardy in terms of weathering. By employing a traditional vocabulary that evolves over the years in response to the climate, the complex is ideally suited to its environment. The large overhangs protect the spaces very efficiently from both sun and rain, while the verandas wrapping around the various units act as climatic buffers. Like the verandas, the open pavilions and walkways admit cooling breezes and generous shafts of light, as well as blurring the boundaries between inside and out, enhancing a sense of interaction with nature.

The interior design and furnishing of the buildings complement the architecture.

Didier Lefort, the interior designer, was involved from the inception of the design process and created some of the architectural details, such as the principal railing that forms a motif throughout the hotel. Local woods have been extensively used in the interiors and, as these woods also form the predominant building material, the interiors pick up the textures of the hotel's structure and the forest beyond, creating a seamless integration between the interiors and the architecture.

The hotel is popular with its clients, providing a sense of luxury and sophistication in a remote natural environment. That this has been achieved with minimal impact on the tropical rainforest is a testament to the responsible and sensitive approach adopted by the architect. In this, and in its development of traditional forms and materials within a modern idiom, the project sets a precedent for others.

Client
Teluk Datai Resorts Sdn Bhd.

Hotel Management
General Hotel Management – Adrian Zecha, President; Jamie Case, General Manager of the Datai Hotel.

Architects
Kerry Hill Architects – Kerry Hill, Principal; Jerry Richard, Associate; Akitek Jururancang Sdn Bhd, Associate Architects.

Interior Architects
Didier Lefort Architects – Didier Lefort and Luc Vaichère; Kumpulan Cipta, Associate Interior Architects – Jay Yeuhen.

Consultants
Rahulan Zain Associates – Rahulan Zain, Structural Engineer; Ranhill Bersekutu Sdn Bhd, Civil and Mechanical Engineering; Nik Farid and Low Sdn Bhd, Quantity Surveyors; Malik Ltd & Associates, Landscape Architects; TSLE AG, Lighting; Malaysian Forest Research Institute – Simmatiri Appanah, Horticulturist and Forest Adviser.

Contractor
Peremba Construction.

Design	1989
Construction	1991–93
Occupation	1993
Site area	220,000m²
Built area	32,850m²
Cost	USD 35,000,000

Bottom left: The site plan shows how the complex is set back from the coast, with only a small beach house on the waterfront itself.

Centre and bottom right: The hotel was carefully positioned to minimize tree felling, and 'pioneering species' were planted to encourage the forest to regenerate quickly.

153

Datai Hotel: Local features were
adopted, such as stilts to protect
against damp and the pavilion form.

Datai Hotel: Eighty-four rooms are
housed in blocks on the ridge, with
views across the forest to the ocean.

155

Datai Hotel: The rooms are connected
by a series of open walkways bathed
in light and air.

Datai Hotel: The guest blocks are
arranged around a swimming pool,
which forms the heart of the complex.

Datai Hotel: Columns of unplaned trees
felled on site create spaces that seem
like extensions of the forest.

Datai Hotel: The siting of the hotel
away from the beach encourages guests
to experience the forest.

Datai Hotel: The interiors show careful attention to detail, using local materials that age gracefully.

CULTIVATING ARCHITECTURE

—

—

—

—

SUHA ÖZKAN

When the Aga Khan Award for Architecture was established in 1977, a set of values that was neither praised, promoted nor respected by prevailing architectural practice was introduced to the wider agenda of architecture in both the urban and rural built environments. It would be incorrect to say that it was exclusively due to the Award that cultural aspects of architecture became a focus in the post-1978 period. However, the new priorities supported by the Award have become the major conceptual tools of the architectural profession.

At the end of the 1970s, when very few were concerned about the 'participation' of people in the formation of their own environment, Hassan Fathy was honoured with the Chairman's Award for his lifelong and dedicated work, based on the participation of local people in building. The technologies and know-how that people inherit as their tradition were cherished, and their methods of construction were put to use through direct participation. Simultaneously, in its first cycle, the Award found the improvement of *de facto* settlements in Indonesia praiseworthy.

This contribution to architectural discourse by the most coveted award to date took the whole profession by surprise. The seeds of 'democratization of the environment' were sown through the Award's serious and meticulous process of selection – a process that discovered, validated and encouraged participation. The following decade saw many eminent thinkers profess that architecture had to become an art that allowed for people's participation in the formation of their futures. The agenda of the architectural media and many development-oriented international agencies began to acknowledge and support 'sustainability' as a guiding principle, defining it in economic, social, environmental and cultural terms. Enriched with many supplementary qualities, this concept substantially enlarged the scope of building activity, especially in the developing world. Accordingly, during subsequent cycles of the Award, sustainability remained an important concern of the juries and became a basic criterion of judgment when validating architectural accomplishments.

This intellectual fabric, woven with ideas that generated awareness and encouraged people's appropriation of their own environments, introduced the new, important concept of 'partnership'. People invested their own human and economic resources, and saw the direct social benefits of their work.

These concepts became the values of a global society concerned with the polar differences between the economically developed and underdeveloped worlds. The new institutions and communication instruments that emerged at the end of the twentieth century established a forum where the problems of each world could be shared by the other. Poverty, along with lack of provision for education and health, became the main concern of the entire planet. Issues such as the protection of human rights, freedom of expression and democratization suddenly took precedence over even politics. In addition, serious environmental problems that could no longer be denied or overlooked required the attention of all, regardless of geography or culture.

In Award seminars, Steering Committee meetings and Master Jury deliberations these widely accepted humanitarian and ethical values have been developed, redefined and propagated within the context of architecture. The industrial and electronic revolutions of the twentieth century bequeathed a legacy of priorities and values that must be administered very wisely today, on the threshold of what will surely be an exciting and productive adventure during the next hundred years. The well-being of mankind and care for the environment have become our top priorities, in great contrast to the immediate past's focus on economic development which, left unchecked, caused damage that may prove irremediable. The equitable distribution of resources to all people is now the most important issue not only architecturally but also, most especially, in terms of human beings caring for each other and their environments.

The widened scope of architecture, reinforced with lessons learnt and noble intentions, has put the Aga Khan Award for Architecture in a unique position to recognize, promote and reward accomplishments. Dedication and the pursuit of continuity have moulded the unique nature of the Aga Khan Award as a 'space for freedom' in search of an 'architecture beyond architecture'. The eight cycles completed over twenty-four years of activity constitute a definition of 'architecture' within the wider context of the built environment, and have consistently promoted nearly all aspects of architecture in Islamic societies today. One of the

Suha Özkan

Award Juries' key considerations remains the future of our architectural heritage. Every jury has tackled this important issue, giving prime consideration to protection and restoration. The main problems addressed in this realm have been the quality of research and the scientific bases and approaches used. All the projects that have received Awards for work in this area have the important component of reviving and developing old building techniques, almost extinct crafts and technical aptitudes.

Ali Qapu, Chehel Sutun and Hasht Behesht, Isfahan, Iran, 1980
Tomb of Shah Rukn-i-'Alam, Multan, Pakistan, 1983
Al-Aqsa Mosque, al-Haram al-Sharif, Jerusalem, 1986
Great Omari Mosque, Sidon, Lebanon, 1989

When the original function of such buildings loses relevance, this should never result in their demolition – even if such destruction could yield great, albeit short-term, economic benefit. Adaptive reuse has been an obvious way to revive our architectural heritage by providing a new existence appropriate to the realities of our time and contemporary conditions. The present Award cycle brings us an entirely new approach, however, with <u>New Life for Old Structures</u> in various locations in Iran. This series of centrally monitored interventions has revived dilapidated and vacant buildings by recycling them for educational and cultural purposes.

The date given for each project indicates the year it received the Aga Khan Award for Architecture.

Rüstem Paşa Caravanserai, Edirne, Turkey, 1980
Historic Sites Development, 1986
Ertegün House, Bodrum, Turkey, 1980
Azem Palace, Damascus, Syria, 1983

Cultivating Architecture

Especially during the period following World War II, fast-growing cities exerted enormous pressure on the historical fabric of their old towns by adopting cheap and inferior construction techniques, with little concern for urban planning and development. Subsequently, new, transient and underprivileged groups moved to these areas. Traditionally, such populations had a lesser sense of a 'history of place' in urban areas, and fewer economic means to cope with the deterioration of the historical heritage. At the same time, many of the international agencies whose mandate was to conserve the historical heritage were primarily preoccupied with monuments; they did not pay particular attention to the urban fabric of old towns until as late as the 1970s. The Award was among the first institutions to recognize contributions towards the safe-keeping and development of this legacy.

In many cities historical housing exists alongside monuments, forming a rich and varied urban fabric, but one that is fragile. Revitalization requires not only architectural restoration but also social and economic infrastructure to ensure community survival and vitality. The Award has successfully identified many examples of such initiatives that have, in turn, engendered and inspired similar efforts in Islamic and non-Islamic communities worldwide.

Conservation of Sidi Bou Saïd, Tunis, Tunisia, 1980
Rehabilitation of Asilah, Morocco, 1989

Conservation of Old Sana'a, Yemen, 1995
Conservation of Mostar Old Town, Bosnia-Herzegovina, 1986
Reconstruction of Hafsia Quarter II, Tunis, Tunisia, 1995
Darb Qirmiz Quarter, Cairo, Egypt, 1983
Restoration of Bukhara Old City, Uzbekistan, 1995
Rehabilitation of Hebron Old Town, Hebron, 1998
Kairouan Conservation Programme, Tunisia, 1992

Suha Özkan

In almost every city in the Muslim world the rapid sprawl of thoughtless and unplanned housing through the urban tissue following the 1950s instilled feelings of surprise and helplessness in architects and decision-makers alike. Spontaneous housing types were attributed popular local names such as 'basti' in the Indian subcontinent, 'kampungs' in Indonesia, 'bidonvilles' in North Africa, 'informal buildings' in Egypt, 'gecekondu' in Turkey and 'refugee camps' in the instance of displaced populations. Architectural theory, practice and education not only disapproved of this form of building activity but also entirely excluded and ignored it. In fact, when the Aga Khan Award embraced and recognized such settlements as essential components of contemporary society, there was initially a public outcry. The Award's pioneering decisions later met with esteem.

Slum Networking of Indore City, Indore, India, 1998
Kampung Kebalen Improvement, Surabaya, Indonesia, 1986
Kampung Improvement Programme, Jakarta, Indonesia, 1980
Kampung Kali Cho-de, Yogyakarta, Indonesia, 1992
Pondok Pesantren Pabelan, Central Java, Indonesia, 1980
Ismaïliyya Development Projects, Ismaïliyya, Egypt, 1986
East Wahdat Upgrading Programme, Amman, Jordan, 1992
Khuda-ki-Basti Incremental Development Scheme, Hyderabad, Pakistan, 1995

Housing has always been a central concern of the Award. In the best examples, families and individuals are embraced by architecture in its most personal sense. Award Juries have explored this subject in many meetings, paying special attention to efforts directed at lower-income groups, be they public or private initiatives. Not enough successful projects have been recognized thus far, but there have been several important accomplishments.

Courtyard Houses, Agadir, Morocco, 1980
Shushtar New Town, Shushtar, Iran, 1986
Dar Lamane Housing Community, Casablanca, Morocco, 1986
Hafsia Quarter, Tunis, Tunisia, 1983
Aranya Community Housing, Indore, India, 1995

165

Rural housing projects identified by the Award have been characterized by ingenious credit mechanisms and simple construction techniques. However, rural development and the architecture appropriate to it have not figured amongst winning projects in the past. For the first time this cycle features rural development alongside rural housing as a priority concern. Three such projects are recognized; each displays an individual approach but, collectively, they stress the undeniable importance of rural life and development. It is within this context that the majority of Muslims lives and works. Aït Iktel, a remote Moroccan village near Abadou, exemplifies an approach that merges development and environmental conservation. In the Tilonia region in India, the Barefoot Architects have developed a humble but meaningful architectural language, while improving living conditions through water harvesting – a programme that provides more time for the education of the rural population, particularly girls and young women. The Kahere Eila Poultry Farming School in Koliagbe, Guinea, displays simple and elegant architectural articulation but also plays an important social role, since its end objective is to increase protein in the diets of Guineans and reduce malnutrition in rural areas.

Grameen Bank Housing Programme, Various locations, Bangladesh, 1989

Mosque architecture has been viewed at many complex levels, and different approaches, reflecting the spirit of Islam and its temporal and geographic plurality have been identified through the Award. The juries have selected a wide range of solutions and architectural expressions, including those that continue vernacular traditions, those that express popular tastes, those that offer classical reinterpretations and those that represent modern creativity.

Great Mosque of Niono, Mali, 1983
Sherefudin's White Mosque, Visoko, Bosnia-Herzegovina, 1983
Yaama Mosque, Yaama, Tahoua, Niger, 1986
Bhong Mosque, Bhong, Rahim-Yar Khan, Pakistan, 1986
Saïd Naum Mosque, Jakarta, Indonesia, 1986
Corniche Mosque, Jeddah, Saudi Arabia, 1989
Mosque of the Grand National Assembly, Ankara, Turkey, 1995
Great Mosque of Riyadh and Redevelopment of the Old City Centre, Riyadh, Saudi Arabia, 1995

Suha Özkan

A commitment to ensuring the continuing relevance of building traditions has not been limited to historical buildings and urban fabric. The Award has also encouraged vernacular building types and technologies that have been developed and transferred from one generation to the next. The most striking example of this type of architecture is the work of the Egyptian architect Hassan Fathy, who received the Chairman's Award in 1980. Since then, most of the juries have continued to identify important facets of vernacular building traditions.

Halawa House, Agamy, Egypt, 1980
Nail Çakırhan Residence, Akyaka Village, Turkey, 1983
Ramses Wissa Wassef Arts Centre, Giza, Egypt, 1983

A continuum within the Award has been the great attention paid to the design and building of projects that respond to their historical, natural and cultural contexts. Many such buildings represent context-ualism in architecture, and have provided significant stimuli for architects and others. The Iraqi architect Rifat Chadirji, a pioneer in the realm of contextualism, received the second Chairman's Award in 1986. In the present cycle, 2001, a Chairman's Award is bestowed upon the Sri Lankan architect Geoffrey Bawa, an influential proponent of an architecture that is environmentally in harmony with tropical contexts. His great talent in creating an architectural language that is fully integrated with its site and place, has been an inspiration to the whole profession in the tropics. Continuing in this tradition is another of this cycle's Award recipients, the Datai Hotel in Pulau Langkawi, Malaysia, designed by the eminent Australian architect Kerry Hill – a project that carries Mr Bawa'ş message to new levels of excellence. In a similar vein, two well-known architects, Jafar Tukan of Jordan and Cengiz Bektaş of Turkey, have demonstrated commitment to contextual architecture in different areas of the Muslim world. The SOS Children's Village in Aqaba, designed by Mr Tukan, and the Olbia Social Centre at Akdeniz Üniversitesi in Antalya, reveal the valour of simplicity, humility and a sensitive understanding of the wider environment. Their work also introduces two new building typologies to this category of winning projects.

Turkish Historical Society, Ankara, Turkey, 1980
National Museum, Doha, Qatar, 1980
Social Security Complex, Istanbul, Turkey, 1986
Gürel Family Summer Residence, Çanakkale, Turkey, 1989
Demir Holiday Village, Bodrum, Turkey, 1992
Medical Centre, Mopti, Mali, 1980

167

Cultivating Architecture

Résidence Andalous, Sousse, Tunisia, 1983
Sidi el-Aloui Primary School, Tunis, Tunisia, 1989
Tanjong Jara Beach Hotel and Rantau Abang Visitors' Centre,
Kuala Trengganu, Malaysia, 1983
Alliance Franco-Sénégalaise, Kaolack, Senegal, 1995
Panafrican Institute for Development, Ouagadougou, Burkina Faso, 1992
Lepers Hospital, Chopda Taluka, India, 1998
Salinger Residence, Selangor, Malaysia, 1998
Mughal Sheraton Hotel, Agra, India, 1980

The development of creative techniques,
building systems and usage of materials
has generated novel architectural expressions. The Award has identified and praised
structural innovation and appropriate use
of materials, as demonstrated by projects
both minor and major in scale.

Kaedi Regional Hospital, Kaedi, Mauritania, 1995
Hajj Terminal, King Abdul Aziz International Airport, Jeddah,
Saudi Arabia, 1983
Stone Building System, Dar'a Province, Syria, 1992
Agricultural Training Centre, Nianing, Senegal, 1980

Suha Özkan

The Award has also recognized the important works of great architects whose creativity, talent and values have set the finest examples. Architects such as Frei Otto, Henning Larsen, Louis I Kahn, Jean Nouvel, Ken Yeang, Omrania, Nayyar Ali Dada and Charles Correa have all been praised. They were able to build in natural and urban environments, whilst enhancing social and cultural values. Their large-scale buildings, approached with modesty and a keen understanding of culture and history, have yielded novel architectural expressions that have been acclaimed locally and internationally.

Ministry of Foreign Affairs, Riyadh, Saudi Arabia, 1989
Intercontinental Hotel and Conference Centre, Mecca, Saudi Arabia, 1980
Water Towers, Kuwait City, Kuwait, 1980
Entrepreneurship Development Institute of India, Ahmedabad, India, 1992
Menara Mesiniaga, Kuala Lumpur, Malaysia, 1995
National Assembly Building, Sher-e-Bangla Nagar, Dhaka, Bangladesh, 1989
Institut du Monde Arabe, Paris, France, 1989
Tuwaiq Palace, Riyadh, Saudi Arabia, 1998
Alhambra Arts Council, Lahore, Pakistan, 1998
Vidhan Bhavan, Bhopal, India, 1998

This cycle, the focus on culture and education has been taken up by the <u>Nubian Museum</u> in Aswan, Egypt, which displays the ethnographic and archaeological heritage of the Nubian population displaced by the construction of the High Dam on the Nile. The sensitive architecture of the complex links the past with the present and connects people with their roots by showcasing their lost heritage. It provides interior and exterior spaces for community gatherings and ensures the continuing vitality of Nubian culture.

Landscapes in which tiring urban life interfaces with the soft, soothing effects of nature have been another of the Award's main concerns. In the past, parks in urban settings and a large reforestation initiative have been commended. In this cycle, an Award has been presented to a large recreational facility – <u>Bagh-e-Ferdowsi</u> in Tehran, Iran – created with a sophisticated use of natural forms and materials. The widely used park offers relief from the urban congestion of Tehran and provides a variety of spaces for social interaction, as well as access to the higher mountain areas.

The Award is now approaching its twenty-fifth anniversary. Thousands of people have contributed talent and intelligence to our endeavour to improve the built environment and, in so doing, to enrich the human condition. In today's electronic age, people can share not only each other's hardships and misery, but also their accomplishments and happiness. The responsible and responsive attitude of the Aga Khan Award for Architecture – to promote successful solutions to difficult problems in the built environment – remains as important today as it was a quarter of a century ago. However, there are many building types, problems and regions that have yet to be addressed. Good buildings for health, industry and housing and schemes to repair both natural and man-made disasters are all areas that the Award must pursue with increasing rigour and determination.

Citra Niaga Urban Development, Samarinda, East Kalimantan, Indonesia, 1989
Palace Parks Programme, Istanbul, Turkey, 1992
Cultural Park for Children, Cairo, Egypt, 1992
Hayy Assafarat Landscaping and al-Kindi Plaza, Riyadh, Saudi Arabia, 1989
Reforestation Programme of the Middle East Technical University, Ankara, Turkey, 1995
Landscaping Integration of the Soekarno-Hatta Airport, Cengkareng, Indonesia, 1995

Suha Özkan

THE 2001 AWARD STEERING COMMITTEE, MASTER JURY AND TECHNICAL REVIEW

The Aga Khan Award for Architecture

Bottom row, left to right: Ali
Shuaibi, Selma al-Radi, Zaha Hadid,
Prince Hussain Aga Khan, His
Highness the Aga Khan, Norani
Othman, Mona Hatoum, Glenn Murcutt.

Middle row: Suha Özkan, Darab
Diba, Zahi Hawass, Doğan Hasol,
Raj Rewal, Kenneth Frampton,
Abdou Filaly-Ansari.

Top row: Luis Monreal, Charles
Correa, Ricardo Legorreta, Azim
Nanji.

The 2001 Award Steering Committee and Master Jury

His Highness the Aga Khan, Chairman.

Selma al-Radi is an Iraqi archaeologist and a research associate at New York University. She has worked in Yemen since 1977. In 1983, she undertook the restoration of the sixteenth-century Madrasa al-Amiriyah in the town of Rada', and is currently overseeing the final phase of the project and the restoration of the internal wall paintings. Also in Yemen, she is completing the rehabilitation of the complex of *Imamate* palaces to house the National Museum in Sana'a, and preparing the catalogue of the museum collections for publication. Dr al-Radi has excavated in Iraq, Egypt, Kuwait, Cyprus, Syria and Yemen, and has published in Arabic and English. She was a Technical Reviewer for the 1986 and 1995 Awards, and was a member of the 1989, 1992 and 1998 Award Steering Committees.

Charles Correa is an Indian architect, planner, activist and theoretician who studied architecture at the Massachusetts Institute of Technology (MIT) and the University of Michigan. He has taught and lectured at many universities, both in India and abroad, including MIT, Harvard University, the University of London and the University of Cambridge, where he was Nehru Professor. He is known for the wide range of his architectural work in India and for his work on urbanization and low-cost shelter in the Third World, which he articulated in his 1985 publication, *The New Landscape*. His architectural designs have been internationally acclaimed and he has received many awards, including the Royal Institute of British Architects Gold Medal in 1984, the Indian Institute of Architects Gold Medal in 1987, the International Union of Architects Gold Medal in 1990, and the Praemium Imperiale for Architecture from the Japan Art Association in 1994. Professor Correa was a member of the 1980, 1983 and 1986 Award Steering Committees and of the 1989 Award Master Jury; he received an Aga Khan Award for Architecture during the 1998 cycle as the architect of Vidhan Bhavan in Bhopal, India.

Kenneth Frampton, British architect and architectural historian, is Ware Professor of Architecture at the Graduate School of Architecture, Planning and Preservation at Columbia University in New York, and is currently a visiting professor at the Academia di Architettura in Menrisio, Switzerland. He trained as an architect at the Architectural Association in London, and has worked as both an architect and an architectural historian. Professor Frampton was a fellow of the Institute for Architecture and Urban Studies, New York, from 1972 to 1982, and a senior tutor at the Royal College of Art, London, from 1974 to 1977. He is the author of numerous influential publications, including *Modern Architecture: A Critical History* (1980, 1985), *Modern Architecture and the Critical Present* (1983), *Modern Architecture: 1851 to 1945* (1981), and *Studies in Tectonic Culture* (1996).

Frank O Gehry, Canadian architect, is the principal in charge of Frank O Gehry and Associates, which he established in 1962. Mr Gehry received his Bachelor of Architecture degree from the University of Southern California and studied city planning at Harvard University Graduate School of Design. His architectural career spans three decades and has produced public and private buildings in America, Japan and, most recently, Europe. His work has been featured in major professional publications and national and international trade journals. In 1986 an exhibition entitled 'The Architecture of Frank O Gehry' travelled throughout North America from Minneapolis to Atlanta, Houston, Toronto and Los Angeles, ending at the Whitney Museum of Modern Art in New York City. In 1989 Mr Gehry was awarded the Pritzker Architecture Prize and was named a trustee of the American Academy in Rome. In 1992 he received the Wolf Prize in Art and the Japan Art Association's Praemium Imperiale for Architecture. Mr Gehry received the first Lillian Gish Award in 1994, the US National Medal of Arts in 1998 and the American Institute of Architecture's Gold Medal in 1999. He served as a member of the 1992 Award Master Jury and the 1995 Award Steering Committee.

Zaha Hadid is a London-based architectural designer whose work encompasses all fields of design, ranging from urban planning through to products, interiors and furniture. She studied architecture at the Architectural Association (AA) in London from 1972, and was awarded the Diploma Prize in 1977. She then became a member of the Office for Metropolitan Architecture (OMA), and began teaching with OMA collaborators Rem Koolhaas and Elia Zenghelis at the AA, where she later led her own studio until 1987. Her work was awarded wide international recognition in 1983, with a winning entry for the Peak, Hong Kong. This success was followed by first-place awards for competitions in Kurfürstendamm, Berlin (1986), for an Art and Media Centre in Düsseldorf (1989), and for the Cardiff Bay Opera House (1994). In 1993, Ms Hadid's fire station for the Vitra furniture company opened to much public acclaim, and the IBA housing scheme in Berlin was completed in the same year. Her paintings and drawings have always been an important testing field, and this work is widely published and shown internationally; major exhibitions have included the 'Deconstructivist Architecture' show at the Museum of Modern Art in New York (1988), the Graduate School of Design at Harvard University (1995), and Grand Central Station in New York (1995). In 1996 Ms Hadid was shortlisted as a finalist for the Victoria and Albert Museum's new Boilerhouse Gallery in London, and for a Philharmonique in Luxembourg. Her office is also joint winner of the Thames Water Habitable Bridge competition. Ongoing projects include a housing scheme in Vienna and projects in London. In 1999 the 'LF One', a pavilion for the Landesgartenschau 1999, opened in Weil am Rhein. Ms Hadid's work was featured in the Master's Section of the 1996 Venice Biennale. She was awarded the Sullivan Chair for 1997 at the University of Chicago School of Architecture, and a guest professorship at the Hochschule for Bildende Kunste in Hamburg. She was a member of the 1998 Award Master Jury.

Luis Monreal, Spanish historian and archaeologist, is currently director general of the Caixa Foundation in Barcelona. From 1985 to 1990 he was the director of the Getty Conservation Institute and oversaw such conservation projects as the tomb of Nefertari in Upper Egypt, the sphinx in Giza, and Buddhist temples in Mogao (Datong, China), as well as other major projects in Cyprus, Jordan, Cambodia and Spain.

From 1974 to 1985 Mr Monreal was the secretary general of the International Council of Museums (ICOM), and was responsible for the establishment or conservation of nine museums throughout the world. He has also served as the curator of the Marés Museum in Barcelona and was a professor of the history of art and museology at the Autonomous University of Barcelona. Mr Monreal has participated in numerous archaeological expeditions, to the High Atlas Mountains in Morocco, Abkanarti in the Sudan, Masmas in Egypt, and Nubia. He is the author of several books on art and archaeology and was a member of the 1995 Award Master Jury and the 1998 Award Steering Committee.

Azim Nanji, specialist in the comparative study of religions, was born in Nairobi, Kenya. He attended schools in Kenya and Tanzania, and Makerere University in Uganda, receiving his masters and doctorate degrees in Islamic Studies from McGill University in Montreal. He has taught at both Canadian and American universities and was the Margaret Gest Professor for the Cross-Cultural Study of Religion at Haverford College, Pennsylvania. Until 1998 he was professor and chair of the University of Florida Department of Religion at Gainesville. Professor Nanji has served as co-chair of the Islam section at the American Academy of Religion, and as a member of the Council on Foundations' Committee on Religion and Philanthropy. In 1998 he was appointed director of the Institute of Ismaili Studies in London. He served as a member of the Master Jury of the 1992 Aga Khan Award for Architecture, and edited a monograph on the Award entitled *Building for Tomorrow*, published by Academy Editions. Professor Nanji was also a member of the 1998 Award Steering Committee.

Ali Shuaibi is a Saudi Arabian architect and planner and co-founder of Beeah Planners, Architects and Engineers, based in Riyadh, with projects in Saudi Arabia, Oman, Yemen, Pakistan and Djibouti. Mr Shuaibi teaches design at King Saud University, and is co-editor of the *Urban Heritage Encyclopaedia*. Several of his projects have received national and international awards, including the al-Kindi Plaza at Hayy Assafarat, the diplomatic quarter in Riyadh, which received an Aga Khan Award for Architecture in 1989 and the Architectural Project Award of the Organization of Arab Towns in 1990. With his office, Beeah, he is currently at work on the National Museum in Riyadh, the Institute of Public Administration in Jeddah and the Embassy of Saudi Arabia in Tunis. Mr Shuaibi was a member of the 1992 Award Master Jury and of the 1995 and 1998 Award Steering Committees.

THE 2001 AWARD STEERING COMMITTEE

Darab Diba is an Iranian architect, trained at the University of Geneva and the Royal Academy of Fine Arts in Liège. Professor Diba teaches theory and history of architecture and conducts design studios at Tehran University's Faculty of Fine Arts. He is also chairman of the Art, Architecture and Urban Planning Department at the Islamic Azad University of Iran. Since 1985 he has been a member of the Iranian Ministry of Higher Education's Central Committee for Academic Architectural Programmes; he has also served as a consultant to the Iranian Ministry of Housing. As an architect in private practice, Professor Diba has built many projects throughout Iran. Widely published, his written works include *La Maison d'Ispahan* (2000), *Contemporary Architecture and Engineering in Iran* (1999), *Principles of Architectural Design* (1985, 1990), and *Art et Nature* (1974). He is also an artist and has organized a number of exhibitions of his sketches, drawings and paintings both in Iran and abroad.

Abdou Filali-Ansary is a Moroccan social scientist and is director of the King Abdul-Aziz Al Saud Foundation for Islamic Studies and Human Sciences in Casablanca. He obtained a doctorate in philosophy from the University of Dijon on the topic of 'The Notion of Intuition in the Philosophy of Spinoza and Bergson' and taught philosophy at the University of Rabat, before becoming secretary general of the University of Mohamed V in Rabat. Since 1994 he has been editor of *Prologues*, a scholarly journal devoted to literature throughout the Maghrib. Mr Filali-Ansary has published numerous articles on contemporary Islamic thought, including the recent essays 'The Challenge of Secularization' (*The Journal of Democracy*, Washington, DC, 1996) and 'Islam and Secularization' (*Revista de Occident*, Madrid, 1997). His monograph entitled *Is Islam Hostile to Secularism?* was published by Editions Le Fennec in 1996.

Doğan Hasol is a Turkish architect, writer and publisher, who trained in architecture at Istanbul Technical University. Dr Hasol participated in the architectural journal *Mimarlık ve Sanat* during its founding years and was later editor-in-chief of *Mimarlık*, the monthly journal of the Turkish Chamber of Architects. From 1965 to 1966 he served as the secretary general of the Istanbul branch of the Turkish Chamber of Architects. He founded Yapı-Endüstri Merkezi (the Turkish Building Centre) with a group of colleagues in 1968, and publishes the monthly architectural review *Yapı*. Dr Hasol is an honorary member of the International Union of Building Centres (UICB), of which he served as president from 1989 to 1995. He is also in private architectural practice in Istanbul. He has written extensively on architecture, including a trilingual dictionary of architecture and building in English, French and Turkish, and an encyclopaedia of architecture. He was made Doctor *honoris causa* by Istanbul Technical University in 1998, and by Yıldız Technical University in 1999.

Mona Hatoum is an artist, born to a Palestinian family in Beirut. Since 1975 she has lived and worked in London, where she studied at Byam Shaw School of Art from 1975 to 1979, and at the Slade School of Art from 1979 to 1981. She has held artist's residencies in Britain, Canada and the United States, and

has taught in London, Maastricht, Paris and Cardiff, where she was senior fellow at the Cardiff Institute of Higher Education from 1989 to 1992. Hatoum's work comprises video, performance, sculpture and installations, creating architectonic spaces that relate to the human body, and dealing with such themes as violence, oppression and the condition of exile. Her work has been exhibited widely in Europe, the United States and Canada. In 1997 a major survey of her work was organized by the Chicago Museum of Contemporary Art, and toured to the New Museum of Contemporary Art in New York, the Museum of Modern Art in Oxford, and the Scottish National Gallery of Modern Art in Edinburgh. Other solo exhibitions have been held at the Centre Georges Pompidou in Paris in 1994 and Castello di Rivoli in Turin in 1999. Hatoum was shortlisted for the prestigious Turner Prize in 1995, and her solo exhibition 'The Entire World as a Foreign Land' was the inaugural exhibition for the launch of Tate Britain in London in 2000.

Zahi Hawass is an Egyptian archaeologist, director general of the Giza pyramids and the Saqqara necropolis. Awarded a Fulbright fellowship, he received his doctorate in Egyptology from the University of Pennsylvania in 1987. On the Giza plateau, Dr Hawass discovered and excavated the tombs of workmen who built the great pyramid of Cheops, and is now excavating a newly discovered pyramid that reveals, for the first time, evidence of the construction techniques of the great pyramids. The excavations have also revealed a pair of previously unknown statues of Rameses II. Dr Hawass directed the conservation of the sphinx, completed in 2000, and is currently working on new approaches towards tourism and archaeology. He is a leading international spokesman on archaeology and Egyptology. He is the author of several monographs on the pyramids, on female royalty in ancient Egypt, and on Egyptology. Dr Hawass is a professor of archaeology at Cairo University and at the University of California at Los Angeles, and frequently lectures at universities throughout the world.

Ricardo Legorreta is a Mexican architect, trained at the Universidad Nacional Autónoma de México. He is the recipient of the Gold Medal of the American Institute of Architects (2000), the Gold Medal of the International Union of Architects (1999), and the Mexican Premio Nacional de las Artes (1992). His architectural work is characterized by the integration of traditional regional architecture and landscapes, with emphasis on light, colour and bold geometry. He has built residences and public facilities throughout Mexico and the south-western United States, including hotels, museums, cathedrals, corporate facilities and science and arts centres. Mr Legorreta lectures extensively throughout the world. He is the author of numerous articles for a wide variety of publications, and a Rizzoli monograph on his work, *Ricardo Legorreta Architects*, was published in 1997. Mr Legorreta served as a member of the Pritzker Architecture Prize Jury from 1983 to 1993.

Glenn Murcutt is an Australian architect, trained at the University of New South Wales, with a private practice in Sydney. Most of his works are domestic residences, set in isolated landscapes throughout Australia, or in urban centres such as Sydney. In 1992 he received the seventh Alvar Aalto Medal in Finland.

He lectures and teaches architecture at universities worldwide. In 1992, he was presented with the Gold Medal of the Royal Australian Institute of Architects (RAIA), and he has been awarded the RAIA's Sir Zelman Cowen Award for Public Buildings on two occasions, in 1994 and in 1999. Made an honorary fellow of the American Institute of Architects and of the Royal Institute of British Architects during 1997, Mr Murcutt received the Richard Neutra International Award for Architecture and Teaching in the United States in 1998, the Green Pin International Award for Architecture and Ecology in Denmark in 1999, and the Kenneth F Brown Asia Pacific Culture and Design Award in the United States in 2000. Mr Murcutt's work is featured in a Thames & Hudson monograph, *Glenn Murcutt: Works and Projects*, by Françoise Fromonot (1995, 1997).

Norani Othman is a Malaysian sociologist and is associate professor and senior fellow at the Institute of Malaysian and International Studies, Universiti Kebangsaan Malaysia. She is a research fellow affiliate at the Institute for Advanced Study in Berlin, where she was also an academic fellow from 1998 to 1999. Professor Othman specializes in social and sociological theory, intellectuals and the intellectual cultures of Third-World societies, Islamic social theory, women's rights, religion and gender studies. She received her MPhil from the University of Oxford in 1982, and was a member of Wolfson College at the University of Oxford from 1980 to 1985. As a Fulbright fellow, she undertook research and a lecture tour on the theme of 'Islam, Women and Human Rights' in the United States during 1996. Professor Othman is vice-president of the Malaysian Social Science Association and a director of the SIS Forum Malaysia Berhad, a Muslim women's organization popularly known as Sisters in Islam. Her work is frequently published in scholarly journals, and she is the editor of *Shari'a Law and the Modern Nation State: A Malaysian Symposium* (1994), *Gender, Culture and Religion: Equal before God, Unequal before Man* (with Cecilia Ng Soon Chim, 1995), and *Malaysia's Experience of Globalization: Actor or Captive?* (with Sumit K Mandal, 2000).

Raj Rewal is an Indian architect and urban design consultant who studied architecture in New Delhi and London. His built works comprise a wide range of building types, and include the Nehru Pavilion, the Scope office complex, the Central Institute of Educational Technology, the World Bank Building, the National Institute of Immunology, the Parliament Library, and the Asian Games Village, all located in New Delhi, India, as well as the Ismaili Centre in Lisbon, Portugal. Mr Rewal's commitment to housing is also central to his built works. In 1989 he was awarded the Gold Medal of the Indian Institute of Architects and the Robert Mathew Award of the Commonwealth Association of Architects. In 1993 he received the Mexican Association of Architects Award, and he is also the recipient of the Great Masters Award of the JK Trust. Mr Rewal's work has been widely exhibited and published, with monographs in English and French; his most recent publication is entitled *Humane Habitat at Low Cost*. He has been a professor at the New Delhi School of Architecture and Planning, and has taught and given lectures at universities in Asia, America and Europe.

THE 2001 AWARD MASTER JURY

Arya Abieta is an Indonesian architect, trained at the Bandung Institute of Technology. He is the founder and director of the architectural firm PT Studio 83 in Jakarta, a member of the conservation committee of the Municipal Jakarta Office for Museums and Preservation, and head of the Indonesian Institute of Architects' Section for Architectural Study and Conservation.

Akram Abu Hamdan is a Jordanian architect in private practice in Amman, trained at the Architectural Association in London. Mr Abu Hamdan directed the architectural research unit at the Jordanian Royal Scientific Society from 1979 to 1982, and was a lecturer and design tutor at the School of Architecture at the University of Jordan for eight years.

Hana Alamuddin is a Lebanese architect, trained at Thames Polytechnic in London and at the Aga Khan Program for Islamic Architecture at the Massachusetts Institute of Technology. She started her own architectural practice, Al-Mimariya, in Lebanon in 1998, and currently has three projects on site and two projects under study. She has been a lecturer at the American University of Beirut since 1994, where she teaches a design studio.

Salma Samar Damluji is an Iraqi architect based in London. She trained at the Architectural Association and the Royal College of Art, and has taught extensively at both institutions. She worked with Hassan Fathy in Cairo, and joined the Human Settlements Division at the United National Economic and Social Commission on West Africa (UNESCWA) in Beirut in 1980. Dr Damluji has conducted major teaching and research projects on the architecture of Hadramut and the towns of south Yemen, and on Moroccan cities.

Dalila ElKerdany is an Egyptian architect and urban planner, trained at Cairo University and the University of California at Berkeley. She is an associate professor of architecture at Cairo University, teaching architecture, design, conservation and urban landscaping, and is in private practice in Cairo with current projects throughout Egypt.

Homeyra Ettehadieh is an Iranian architect. She trained at the École des Beaux Arts in Paris, and worked in architectural offices in Paris and Montreal prior to returning to Tehran in 1989. She has undertaken studies on the old centre of Tehran, and has collaborated on studies of traditional architecture. She is managing director and chief architect of Y Ettehadieh & Partners Consulting Architects and Engineers.

Omar A Hallaj is a Syrian architect in private practice in Aleppo, trained at the University of Texas at Austin. He is a partner in the Suradec Consortium for Sustainable Urban Rehabilitation, Architectural Design and Engineering. Mr Hallaj is also a consultant for the rehabilitation of the old city of Aleppo, where he is preparing detailed local plans and supervising implementation procedures for developing historical neighbourhoods.

Khadija Jamal is a Pakistani architect and planner, trained at the Aga Khan Program for Islamic Architecture at the Massachusetts Institute of Technology and the NED University of Engineering and Technology in Karachi. Ms Jamal is an associate partner in the Consultants Group, an architecture and planning firm. She is a visiting faculty member of the Department of Architecture at Dawood College of Engineering and Technology, and serves as honorary director of the Aga Khan Rural Support Programme and the Baltit Heritage Trust.

Romi Khosla is an Indian architect who received a Bachelor of Economics degree from the University of Cambridge and qualified as an architect at the Architectural Association in London. He founded the Group for Rural and Urban Planning (GRUP) in Delhi in 1974. His recent work includes developmental and revitalization projects for the United Nations Development Programme (UNDP) in Central Asia, Tibet, Egypt, Bulgaria, Romania, Kosovo, Palestine and Cyprus, and for the government of India in the Himalayan belt.

Jolyon Leslie is a South African architect, trained at the University of Cambridge. He has worked extensively in post-disaster and post-war reconstruction in the Middle East and in Asia. The focus of his professional work has been largely in Islamic societies, where he has explored ways in which the built environment can foster processes of social development, particularly within marginal communities.

Rahul Mehrotra is an Indian architect, trained at the Ahmedabad School of Architecture and at Harvard University. He established his private practice in 1990, and is the executive director of the Urban Design Research Institute, which promotes research on the city of Bombay with the aim of influencing urban design policy.

Ralph Mills-Tettey is a Ghanaian architect, trained at the University of Science and Technology in Kumasi. From 1977 to 1997 Professor Mills-Tettey lectured at the University of Ife, Nigeria, becoming professor of architecture and dean of the Faculty of Environmental Design from 1995 to 1997. He returned to Ghana in 1997 where he is a consulting architect specializing in housing, urban development and educational buildings.

Ashraf M A Salama is a practising Egyptian architect, trained at Al-Azhar University and North Carolina State University. He is associate professor of architecture at Al-Azhar University, as well as chairman of the Department of Architecture at Misr International University. Dr Salama serves as a consultant to the Egyptian Ministries of Housing, Tourism and Culture, and is a member of the UIA/UNESCO Architectural Education Committee.

Fernando Varanda is a Portuguese architect. He graduated in architecture from the Lisbon School of Fine Arts, receiving his Master's degree from New York University and his PhD from Durham University. He is currently a professor in the Department of Urbanism at the Universidade Lusófona in Lisbon. Since 1973 he has undertaken extensive research on built spaces in Yemen, published in both monographs and specialist publications. Professor Varanda is also in private practice in Lisbon.

Ayşil Yavuz is a Turkish restoration architect, with doctorate degrees in conservation from the University of Rome and from Istanbul Technical University. She has been a staff member since the foundation of the Department of Restoration at Middle East Technical University in Ankara, where she also teaches restoration design and historical structural systems, and serves as a thesis director for Master's and doctoral students. Professor Yavuz was the chair of the Department of Interior Architecture at King Faisal University, Damman, Saudi Arabia, from 1982 to 1986.

Yıldırım Yavuz is a Turkish architect and instructor and dean of the Middle East Technical University (METU) Faculty of Architecture. Professor Yavuz received Bachelor's and Master's degrees in architecture from METU, and a second Master's degree in architecture from the University of Pennsylvania. From 1962 to 1982 he taught architectural design and history at METU; from 1982 to 1986 he taught design and history of architecture at King Faisal University, Damman, Saudi Arabia; and from 1988 to 1994, he was vice-dean of the Faculty of Art, Design and Architecture at Bilkent University, Ankara.

THE 2001 AWARD TECHNICAL REVIEW

Suha Özkan, Secretary General, has been associated
with the Aga Khan Award for Architecture since
1983. Having studied architecture at the Middle East
Technical University (METU) in Ankara, he went to the
Architectural Association in London to study
theory of design. He taught architectural design and
design theory at METU for fifteen years, becoming
associate dean of the Faculty of Architecture in 1978
and vice-president of the University in 1979. On behalf
of the Aga Khan Trust for Culture he has organized
two international architectural competitions – for
the Revitalization of Samarkand, Uzbekistan (1991),
and for the new Museum of Islamic Arts in Doha,
Qatar (1997).

Shiraz Allibhai, Education Officer, the Aga Khan
Trust for Culture
Marco Christov, Documentation Architect
Farrokh Derakhshani, Director of Award Procedures
Sandrine Ducrest, Documentation Architect
Jack Kennedy, Executive Officer
William O'Reilly, Librarian, the Aga Khan Trust
for Culture
Françoise Rybin, Executive Secretary
Karen Stylianoudis, Award Procedures Secretary

The Aga Khan Award for Architecture
P.O. Box 2049
1211 Geneva 2
Switzerland
www.akdn.org

THE AWARD SECRETARIAT

176

The Aga Khan Award for Architecture